T0368544

The Seventh Angel

A dream journal & transformational guide into the world of lucid dreaming

Jerimiah Molfese

AuthorHouse™
1663 Liberty Drive
Bloomington, IN 47403
www.authorhouse.com
Phone: 833-262-8899

This book is printed on acid-free paper.

ISBN: 978-1-6655-4401-6 (sc)
ISBN: 978-1-6655-4402-3 (e)

Print information available on the last page.

Published by AuthorHouse 11/11/2021

authorHOUSE®

GOING ON A
WALKABOUT THROUGH
DREAMTIME

To my readers,

This book was made from my real lucid dream experiences. I have hundreds of lucid dreams and all the different places that I have been is portrait in The Seventh Angle. When you are in a lucid dream there are many types of guidance from dream characters to your own intuition. In many lucid dreams you will have many voices guiding you as you battle your dream and try to complete your intention that you want to accomplish. As you get good at lucid dreaming you will find that in all lucid dreams the dream is trying to stop you from accomplishing what you intend to do, very similar to waking life. I wrote this book with the intention for the reader to get a good understanding of the possibilities and type of place one can go in the dream world while portraying the incredible concept of becoming an angle as a human using lucid dreaming directed thinking and listing to our high intuition. As you read throughout this book please keep in mind that in the lucid dream state one can have many different voices and guidance from different places and it is my goal to give you the reader a bit of experiences throughout this book of what that might be like.

Go to http://www.hidreamers.com
to get some free gifts I have prepared for you.

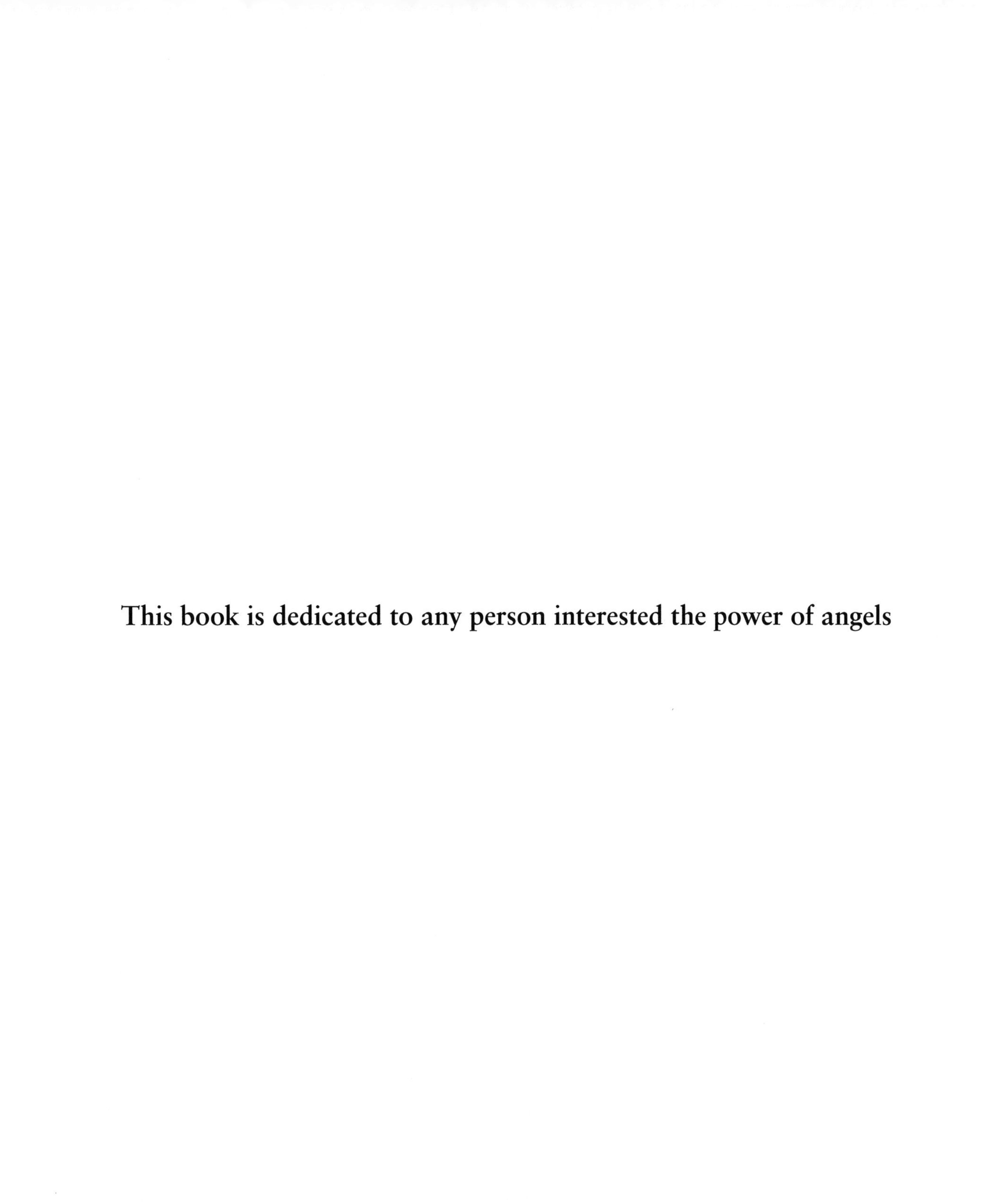
This book is dedicated to any person interested the power of angels

Contents

Acknowledgments

I would like to thank Valerie Gautreaux
for being a great friend and editor.
I could not have finished the book with out
the help she gave.

Chapter 1
The journey begins

CHAPTER 1

THE JOURNEY BEGINS

"These experiments are very important to the welfare of all life on earth," my father said with a seriousness I'd seen many times before.

In spite of his profound words, I didn't understand what was so important about depriving a person of his senses in a flotation chamber, then flashing lights at him when he started to dream. The one hundred thousand dollar grant that Stanford University gave my father was a miracle, considering that the scientists here in California, and especially at Stanford, thought that my father was crazy. They considered the experiments that he was conducting on the lucid dream state as a waste of good grant money because the subject had no relationship to real science, and didn't hesitate to say that the money could be used to conduct real experiments on real science.

Personally, I found the experiments in lucid dreaming quite interesting. A person in the lucid dream state knows that he's dreaming when he's in a dream. When he reaches this state of lucid awareness in the dream, he can change the dream and control it in any way he wishes.

My father had told me that, in the dream state, he was traveling through different worlds in a dimension that was different than the one I was in at that moment, saying, "Seth, it's important for you to know that this place we call earth is much larger than what meets the eye. Don't ever forget that."

The other scientists were saying that my father's experiments were nothing more than a person going into a world of illusions created by different fragments of memory that arrange themselves as a dream, and that world appears to be real to the dreamer. They said that my father was becoming lucid within his own mind, creating a world of past memories.

There I was, earning extra college credits assisting a loony scientist who thought he was traveling through different dimensions, opening new doors for humanity, when he was really only playing around with the imagination of the human brain, and not going anywhere beyond his own mind. And that loony scientist was my father!

The EEG machine, hooked to my father's head by electrodes, was reading his brain waves. The printout showed me that he was dreaming, and I knew it was time. Just before he went into the floatation tank, he said, "Son, when the EEG shows that I'm in the REM (Rapid Eye Movement) stage of sleep, press this green button e." A soft flash of light would be sent to my father every second. "And don't forget to wake me at exactly ninety minutes from onset of sleep," I remembered him saying as I pressed the green button.

I looked up in the direction my climbing partner went, and yelled as loud as I could, "I can't make it!"

I heard nothing. He had gone out of sight. I tried yelling even louder, "I can't make it!" No reply.

I realized I was stranded alone over a hundred feet up in the air. Paralyzing fear struck my body like a bolt of lightning as I thought, "I can't move. I'm going to fall soon."

I screamed even louder, "I can't make it and I'm going to fall!!" Silence.

I knew I needed help or I was going to die. I looked down and wondered how the hell I'd gotten up here with no ropes and no climbing partner.

Flash. A bright light illuminated all around me. "What is that?" I thought. I covered my eyes.

Flash. There it was again. Flash. One more time.

Suddenly I realized that I'd done it! "I'm dreaming!" I said to myself. I saw the light flash again, reassuring me that I was in a dream. My fear of falling disappeared because I knew I was dreaming, and that's why I didn't know how I got there.

I realized that the flashing light (as another flash brightened the air around me again) is the signal to let me know that I'm dreaming. The lights are my dream sign.

I jumped into the air and began to fly, remembering that I was in a plane of existence where there is no time, distance, or gravity. This plane is a thought-built region and I only have to think and feel what I want, and it will happen instantly.

The sensation of flying in the air was magnificent! I could feel the air on my face, and smell it as it moved gently across my nose. It seemed so real. It was real. I was dreaming. I was lucid dreaming, flying in another dimension on a whole different plane of existence than the earth's plane. I felt like the first person to walk on the moon.

The moon. "The moon", I thought again, and there it was, the most brilliant and brightest moon I'd ever seen. I landed on a rock to get a good look at the moon and thought, "This is a dream, and I have an intention to accomplish. My intention is to find the girl." I tried to remember what she looked like and what her name was. Then it came to me. Her name was Amber. I yelled it out loud. "Amber, come to me. Amber, I need to see you!"

I closed my eyes, concentrated, and yelled as loud as I could, "Amber, where are you?"

"Jamie, look behind you."

The voice. That was the voice! I slowly turned around. Clouds began to form into a big, swirling storm moving in my direction. I was startled, but then remembered that this was a dream and I would wake up if I wasn't careful with my feelings.

"Good, Jamie. "Very good."

That voice again. The clouds swirled like a small tornado, changing every second, eventually transforming into . . .

"Amber, is that you?" "Yes, Jamie it's me."

"I knew that you would come if I asked. I see that you're wearing the symbol on your necklace." "Yes," she replied.

"The last time we met, you were wearing the symbol. That's why I wanted to call you back. The symbol is very important to me and my work back on earth."

I looked directly at her and asked, "Amber, what's the password to the path of spirituality?"

She looked directly at me and replied, "GOODNESS ALONE
IS POWER."

"That's it! You're a member - you really are!"

"Yes, I'm a member. Now come along. We have much work to do."

"Jamie! Jamie, wake up, wake up!" I tapped my father on his shoulder. He opened his eyes and looked at me.

"It's been exactly ninety minutes," I said, looking into his eyes and making sure he was awake.

"How did it go? Did you get to that fourth dimension you're always talking about?"

"Yes, now please hand me the tape recorder." I knew I should never interrupt when he's recording his dreams. He insisted that the dream experience be recorded immediately upon waking up so that as much of the dream could be remembered and original.

But I couldn't wait, and asked, "So, what happened?"

"It was a breakthrough, Seth! I did it! I finally did it! I saw Amber, and she was as beautiful as ever."

"Dad, I know you're infatuated with Amber, but you can't replace Mom with some dream girl." I looked at him with concern, wondering if my father really was crazy.

"Listen son, I know that things have been hard since your mother died, but we need to get on with our lives. It's been three years and we should just forget about her. She's gone."

"You are infatuated with this girl Amber, aren't you," I said sadly.

"Seth, listen. I know that you think I'm going crazy searching out strange and beautiful girls in my dreams, but I'm not. One day you'll see that this work is very important to the future of mankind," My Dad said with a seriousness that made me uncomfortable.

Not changing his expression, he said, "Come here and sit down. I want to explain something to you." I moved over and sat beside him.

"Seth, you're twenty years old. I know you and have better things to do with your time than help your old father in his crazy experiments, but I need you right now. You're the only person who will stand by me in my research in lucid dreaming."

"I know, Dad, but. . .," I began, but he interrupted me. "But nothing. I know that you think I'm replacing your mother with Amber, but that's not the case. You see, Seth, Amber is the one. She's wearing the symbol and she knew the password to the true path of spirituality. Do you remember when you were young and I would read those stories to you as you fell asleep?"

"Yes, but what does that have to do with Mom and Amber?" "Those stories were ancient myth from the time of Atlantis.

They're the foundation of the spiritual path to enlightenment. I know that you think that they're just old stories for bedtime, but they're more, much more, as you'll see."

"Whatever you say, Dad," I said, still pretty confused.

He continued, almost urgently. "The secrets of spiritual alchemy are taught within the text that was read to you as a boy, and when you get older you may understand the power of spiritual transformation."

"Spiritual transformation. It's all very interesting, but I need to get to my science class or I'll be late. Let's chat about spiritual transformation over dinner, OK?" I said, feeling that I was putting him off, but I couldn't be late for class.

"OK son, get to class. And remember that I love you even if you won't listen to my theories." His voice was almost sorrowful.

"Dad, it's not that I'm not interested. I just have to go!" "I know. Get going. We can talk about it over dinner"

I left the room with a strange feeling in my gut, like something was wrong.

"That smells wonderful! I'm starving! That science class was so boring. It was like it sucked not only my intelligence out, but my lunch too! I don't understand what balancing an egg on a table has to do with science." I reached over my Dad's shoulder to dip a finger into the pasta sauce that was simmering on the stove.

"Seth, all things are science, and one day you'll learn to appreciate that. It's the balance of the positive and negative forces that allow you and me to be having this conversation. So the experiment of balancing an egg may be boring, but it's a good metaphor for the creation of all life, on this dimension at least," he said with a small smile on his face.

"Don't give me the 'all things are science 'talk again," I laugh. "Tell me about Amber. I know that you think I don't care about your experiments, but I do. As a matter of a fact, I started to have my own lucid dreams about a week ago."

My father turned to look at me, pride in his eyes. "That's great, son! I knew if you wanted to you could do it! So now you can understand what I'm talking about."

"Don't worry, I believe you. I know now that the lucid dream world is real. If any of those closed-minded scientists would put some effort into having a lucid dream, they'd believe it too. Having lucid dreams has changed my whole view on science. It's opened my eyes to the idea that this world is much larger than we think, like you always said. Now don't hold out on me, tell about Amber," I said as we sat down at the kitchen table to eat dinner.

"Well, like I said earlier, she was wearing the symbol around her neck and she knew the password to the path of spirituality. Do

you know what that means, son?"

"No."

"It means it's time to celebrate because I finally did it! I finally contacted someone who can help me understand the process of spiritual transformation, very much like the ancient alchemists would take different metals from the earth and combine them in the right manner to make gold. One day, Seth, you'll remember your spiritual path, and obtain enlightenment like no other person has." My father was really excited.

"I don't understand. You want Amber to show you how to transform metal into gold? Is that what this is about - money? I thought that you were talking about spiritual transformation, not the transformation of your pocketbook!" I was getting angry.

"Now wait a minute. You don't understand. It wasn't the gold that was important to the ancients. It was the process of making it that was important. The next time I meet Amber I'll ask her to help me in the process of acquiring spiritual gold, not metal gold." "Spiritual gold - what's that?" I asked.

"The ancients sought the spiritual transformation of their character in order to reach a state of spirituality where it's possible

to build a spiritual body. That spiritual body is the 'gold'."

"How can a body be gold?"

"Seth, remember where you are and what you're doing right now, and you might have a clue. It's not gold like you think of the metal gold. This is spiritual gold. It's a different king of spiritual body, a body that never dies. This is the key to life: the ability to transform the human character into a body that combines with the power of unity to create an angel. That's what this is all about, son - angels." My Dad was almost whispering as he explained his mission.

"Angels? You want to become an angel? What happens then?" I almost couldn't believe I was hearing him.

He continued, talking slowly. "The ancients believed that after properly transforming your character to express as pure spirituality, and adding the ingredient of unity, an angel is formed. And as an angel you can perform your great work."

"What's my great work?"

"It nothing like work you're used to doing. This kind of work you love to do, and it's part of God's great plan. You essentially become one with God, and help to fulfill the plan." We'd finished the pasta and salad, and I barely remembered eating. I was fascinated at what my father was telling me, in spite of my doubts.

"Here, I want you to have this," Jamie said, reaching into his pants pocket. He pulled out a necklace - it was identical to the one he was wearing. "It was your mother's. I meant to get you one of your own, but now it would be right for you to have your mother's."

He got up and came over to me, placing the necklace around my neck. I could feel the energy coming from it, and it soothed my heart, lifting the grief I'd felt ever since my mother died.

"Thanks, Dad! I'll honor it with my life," I said, with gratitude and love for this man.

"I hope you'll do much more than that, Seth," my father said, smiling but still very serious. "I want you to learn the meaning of the symbol and remember what your inner power is. Try to get connected with the power that God gave you, and maybe one day you can follow in my steps and continue the work I've in proving that the fourth dimension is real."

"I would like very much to do that, Dad."

"I hoped you would, Seth," he said, looking deep into my eyes. "But enough talk about science. Let's go to bed - I'm beat."

I stood up, and again had a terrible feeling that something bad was going to happen. I looked at my father and said, """I love you, Dad, and I'll learn to follow in your steps. You're a brilliant scientist. Good night."

"Good night, son. And have some lucid dreams tonight."

I lay in my bed and started doing the exercise my Dad had taught me to enter a lucid dream while still awake. My father didn't know how greatly I was interested in lucid dreaming, or that I had practiced the exercises to the point where I could enter the lucid dream state by will. I wasn't keeping this from him. I had realized only the past few days that I could enter a lucid dream by will by using a combination of exercises.

As I relaxed my body, I visualized a ball of light within my third eye, feeling the power of my pituitary gland 'opening'. Different images and patterns of the dream world began to appear around me. My father had told me that this is the hypnogogic state of sleep, which means that the dream state is close at hand.

I visualized my hands (my dream hands) in front of me, mentally flipping them over from front to back, as I counted, "One I'm dreaming, two I'm dreaming", and so on up to one hundred. Then I started over from one. I knew that if I concentrated on my third eye, and didn't wander into sleep, I would enter the dream state soon.

Then I saw a mirror in front of me, and I could see my reflection in it. I thought,

As the ball of light filled my body with warmth, I concentrated on my reflection and my third eye at the same time. Then it started. I was spinning and being pulled from my stomach. Even though many people get frightened when these sensations happen by wake induced lucid dreaming or by walking into the dream world consciously, I thought it was exciting. I knew that if I just relaxed and stayed calm, I would come out of my body.

I began to float up into the air, and the sensation of being released from my body was almost overwhelming.

"Stay relaxed and concentrate, Seth." "Who said that?" I thought.

Silence.

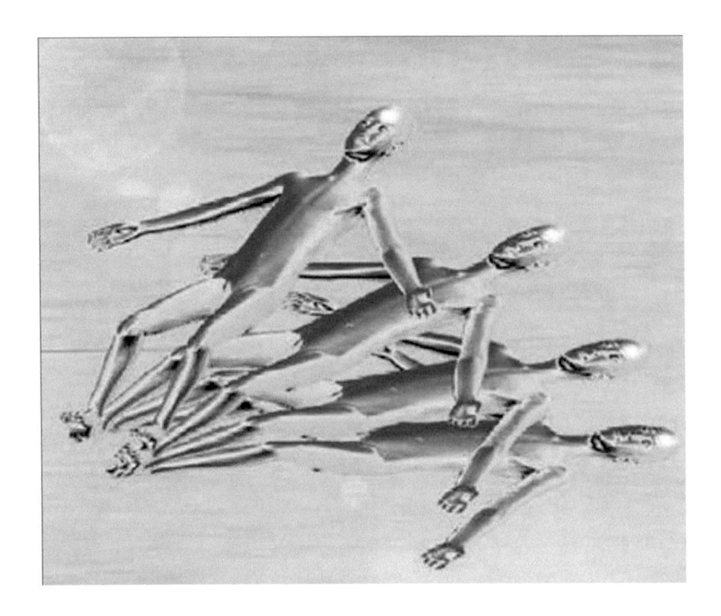

I was floating above my body. I looked down and saw myself in my bed. I knew then that I could enter the dream state. I thought, "I'm dreaming! I did it, and it's wonderful! I'm dreaming."

I thought, "What do I want to do?" Space. That's it. I thought I'd fly to space and back. I began to fly up toward the skylight in the ceiling of my bedroom, seeing the blue sky on the other side of it. I remembered that I should go through the window gracefully, not fast or hard; or I would just crash into it. I moved with grace, my hands touching the window, and the glass bubbled as my fingers moved through it, like dipping into a pool of water. As I slowly moved through the window, my body was filled with a buzzing and tingling feeling.

"Don't let it wake you, Seth."

That voice again. Whatever and wherever it was, it was right. I had to keep my emotions under control or I'd wake up. I was halfway through the window now and the buzzing and tingling grew stronger as my legs, then my feet passed through the glass with a pop. Hovering above the window, I tried to figure out where the voice came. I looked up at the sky, seeing the clouds swirling around very fast. I thought, "Everything in the dream world is so vivid and wonderful, so full of beauty. Is this place real? Am I in another reality?"

"Yes." The voice.

"Who are you?" I said out loud. "Who are you, Seth?"

"Who am I? I'm Seth."

"And I'm Seth," the voice replied, closer this time.

"If you're Seth and I'm Seth, then that means you are me." "Yes." This time the voice was right in my ear.

"But how can you be me?" I wondered.

At that moment, a 3-D screen appeared in front of me, and on it was my father reading the myth of the twin souls to me.

"I'm you and you're me. I remember now," I said. "You're part of me. My higher self. My twin. My Dad calls it our counterpart. He said that everything and everyone on earth has a counterpart that exists in the fourth dimension. You're my higher self. You're here to guide me as I journey through this unknown land."

I put my hands out in front of me and flew as fast as I could toward the clouds. I felt the wind pass over me. I was flying toward a big cloud. It began to change as I passed through it, transforming into hundreds of clear, perfect spheres that spiraled up as I flew by. I felt a tingling in my body that spiraled up from my feet and out through my head and connected me to the clouds. Then I was floating in the blackness of space. It was just like I imagined, an infinite number of stars and empty space.

Slam.

A wall of beautiful patterns and color was swirling all around me. I remembered that I had to move gracefully though the skylight window, and thought that I should do the same with this wall of patterns.

"Seth, do it with grace. You must use your feelings to guide you now," I hear from my higher self. I thought of what it felt like to be held by my mother as a child, and the most peaceful feeling entered my body. As I started to pass through the wall of patterns and colors, I wondered if this space was in the fourth dimension.

My hands went through the wall, then my head. It was very strange to feel part of my body one place and the other part experiencing something else in another place. I was amazed to see planets moving quickly by on the other side. There were planets filled with color and planets that were totally black. Using all my concentration to move my legs out of the old world and into the new world, I flew toward one of the planets made of color. The next thing I knew I was on top of what appeared to be the Empire State building, looking out over a city, thinking, "What is reality - this world, or the world my father is in right now?"

"Seth, stop playing around. It's time to learn what you've come to this place to learn," my higher self said.

"What would that be?"

"How to apply intention and carry it out in the dream world, as a start. Everything in this place is based on your thoughts and emotions; therefore, you must practice the art of directed thinking and induced emotion if you want to do anything here."

"What do you mean 'do anything'? Didn't you see how I just went through that wall of patterns or whatever it was? That wasn't easy, you know. It took a lot of directed thinking and induced emotion," I replied, a little defensively, wondering where I'd heard the terms 'directed thinking and induced emotion' before.

A movement to my left caught my attention, and I saw a little mouse moving slowly toward me squeaking faintly at me. The squeaking got louder as the mouse got closer. Then the squeaking became a beeping sound.

My alarm was waking me up.

I opened my eyes, feeling very excited that I could do anything I wanted. I was on top of the world. It almost seemed that the physical world was an illusion and my dream world was where I really belonged.

I jumped out of bed and wrote the whole experience down in my dream journal, trying to understand the importance of directed thinking and induced emotion to the work I was to do in the dream world.

As I went downstairs toward the kitchen, the feeling of dread that I had the night before when I said good night to my father returned. The kitchen was dark and empty. Strange - Dad was always up before me, cooking breakfast. A cold chill ran up my spine.

I switched on the kitchen light. A note with my name on it lay on top of a book on the table. It read: "Seth, after our talk last night I thought it would be a good idea for you to start reading about how to control your thoughts and emotions by will so that you will have the ability to remember where you are. This will give you the knowledge to travel through the dream world successfully. If you're really interested in following in my steps and helping me prove that there is an alternate reality, I guarantee it is much more interesting than balancing an egg on a table. Love, Jamie."

The book was titled Mental Alchemy - Success Through the Art of Directed Thinking and Induced Emotion. I realized that I'd heard this term in my dream last night and thought, "Dad will think this is great!"

Going toward his bedroom door, the feeling of deep dread crept back into the depths of my gut, really strong this time. Tears welled up in my eyes. Time stopped.

"Dad, what are you doing in there? You need to get up." I called at his door.

No answer.

"Dad, are you in there?" Silence.

I knew something was terribly wrong as I opened the door.

My father lay on his bed, eyes closed, not moving.

"Dad, are you OK?" I put my hand on his cheek. He felt cool. Too cool.

"Dad are you . . . .," I began, then stopped, shock overtaking my body.

"NO! Dad, please be OK!" I shook his shoulder. He was stiff and cold, and that brought it to my full attention. My father was dead.

"Seth, it will be OK."

The voice of my dream! The voice of my dream is here, too!

Overwhelmed by confusion and sorrow, I stood next to my dead father and realized that I was truly alone forever.

Chapter 2
The diary

CHAPTER 2

THE DIARY

The bright light of the full moon beams through my bedroom window and onto my face as I lie in my bed thinking about how much I miss my father. The power of the moon fills me with love as if I was her baby in its crib. I know this is a very special night. I feel magic in the air.

I get out of bed and move my tired body to the bathroom. I stare into the mirror and instantly feel like I'm in a trance, mesmerized by the reflection of my own eyes. In the pupil of my eyes I see myself lying in my bed.

That's strange. Maybe this is a dream.

The next second I'm in my bed. I feel a buzzing sensation around my body, something I've never felt before or after a lucid dream.

I glance out the window at the full moon. I look at my hands, flip them over once, and realize that I'm still dreaming. I never woke up! I jump out of bed, turn around, and see myself lying in my bed. I'm excited and amazed at this false awakening. Looking at my hands again I say aloud, "This is a dream", trying to become fully aware of my state. As I become more lucid, I remember my intention: Amber. I must find Amber.

With more focus this time, I look out the window, again directing my thoughts out far beyond it. I imagine what it feels like to fly through the window, and in the next instant I'm doing just that. Knowing that I must control my excitement at the sensation of flying or I'll wake myself up from the dream, I stay calm and concentrate on my intention of finding Amber, focusing on what I know about her. Mentally I call to her, beckoning her to come to me, even though I have no idea what she looks like or what her energy is like.

"Amber! Amber I need to contact you," I yell out loud. I listen for a response, but hear nothing. Then I hear my higher self say, "Seth, you must gain rapport with Amber if you want to contact her."

Rapport? How do I gain rapport with her if I don't know what she feels like? I've never even seen her!

"The answer lies with your father," my higher self replies.

But my father has passed on. How can I know about Amber from him?

I hear a loud rumbling sound in the distance, and turn to see clouds swirling around, lightening crashing within them. A powerful storm is moving toward me. The sound of it makes me think that something very strange is going to happen. Bracing myself against the wind, I stare straight into the swirling clouds and lightening, wondering why this storm is in my lucid dream and why it's racing so fast toward me.

"Seth, hold on and concentrate if you don't want to wake up," my higher self-shouts.

What do you mean, 'hold on'?! I'm dreaming and I know I have the power to control this dream, so the storm won't wake me up.

"There are things in the dream world that we can control, but weather is not one of them! So prepare yourself if you don't want to wake up!"

I wonder what kind of weather is in the fourth dimension.

The storm strikes me, and I feel physically sick, as if a disease has taken me over. The wind swirls and the lightning flashes all around me as the storm moves over my body. I'm in the center of a powerful energy that overwhelms my concentration. The storm is more powerful than I am, and I wonder what kind of energy in the fourth dimension could be so powerful that it isn't influenced by directed thinking and induced emotion.

I wake up in my bed instantly grabbing my tape recorder.

Recording 1/2/1999 - 2:50 a.m

The lucid dream I just had confused me because I have no idea what kind of power is in the fourth dimension. I need to understand how what kind of weather can be powerful enough to not be swayed by my thoughts and emotions, and to make me feel so sick. Also, if I have to gain rapport with Amber in order to find her, I don't know how to do that when I don't even know her. My higher self said that my father has the answers to these questions but he's dead and I don't know how to contact him. I'm at a loss. How can I continue on my journey if I can't get the answers to my questions?

I stop recording. I'm really confused. Suddenly I remember that my father kept a diary of everything he did, and in full detail.

It should contain something about Amber that I can use to gain rapport with her. Welcome calm washes over me. I get out of bed and go to the closet where I keep a special chest of my father's records of all the experiments we did together before he passed on.

"Seth, is this a dream?" I hear from my higher self.

A dream? I test my state of consciousness by looking at the door to the closet, then looking away for a moment. When I look at the door again, it hasn't changed. If I were dreaming, the door would have changed. This state test tells me that I'm awake.

"No, I'm not dreaming," I reply. "Why the question?"

"Do you remember your father telling you about the start of a new awakening? Think about that as you open that chest."

When my higher self speaks, I take it seriously. I think very deeply about whether this is a dream or not, and open the chest. The diary is on top of the records of the experiments we did together. As I take it in my hand, I feel its energy, warm and alive. Lying back on my bed, I glance through the diary. Every experience my father had of traveling through the fourth dimension is documented in detail and full explanation. On the cover are certain page numbers, some with the word 'Amber 'written next to them, and some with the phrase 'inner plane weather 'written next to them.

"Seth, your father wrote down those specific page numbers for you," my higher self explains. "As we go through these entries one by one, I'll help you with the translation as it pertains to your journey."

Excited, I quickly go to page 22, which is the first page listed on the diary's cover as 'Page 22 - Amber'- my father's first experience with Amber. The entry is dated January 1, 1969. Before I was born.

January 1, 1969.

I was lying on my bed, relaxing my body and preparing to come out of my body into the dream world. I had set my intention to contact a higher being who had a strong spiritual philosophy, and ask it to teach and guide me on my journey through life. The next thing I knew, I was standing next to my body that was lying on my bed.

The amazement of being in the dream world is always very strong, but I stayed calm by focusing on my intention. I sat in a meditation pose with my legs crossed, my hands on my knees, fingers touching, eyes closed, and began to meditate in the dream world. Instantly, I was surrounded by brilliant colors. It was like sitting in the middle of a rainbow. I felt very small. My intention was strong and I knew that I was dreaming. I asked aloud, "Will a spiritual being come and guide me on my journey through life?" I repeated the question a few times, keeping my feeling strong and coming from my heart

When I opened my eyes, I wasn't in my room any more. I was looking at a beautiful city made of golden light. Energy was beaming outward in all directions of this city, and I could feel its spiritual energy flowing through my body. The city glowed like the sun.

I sat watching in awe, wondering if I had raised my vibratory state to a place of pure spirituality. Then a flash of light came from the center of the city, and a ray of colored light came straight up out of the flash, filling the sky with beautiful color. As spiritual energy spread throughout everything, the sky was filled with beautiful colors. A small ball of light dropped from the sky, reflecting everything around it, and stopped right in front of me. I stared into it, seeing my face reflected in it. As I looked into my eyes, I saw a little baby. Then there was a huge flash, and, instead of my own eyes, I was staring into the eyes of the most beautiful woman I'd ever seen.

She stood there, naked, reflecting pure spiritual energy. Her beauty spread throughout my entire body. As we stared into each other's eyes, the intensity of her energy began to wake me up. I resisted with all my power, but the dream began to slip away.

I woke up with one very strong thought: He's coming. He's coming.

"Seth, that baby is you," I hear from my higher self.

I look up from my father's diary. Me? What does it mean? My father never said anything about this to me, and we were very close. He would surely have said something to me about this experience. I flip through the pages of his diary and find an entry titled 'Inner Plane Weather', dated February 25, 1988.

February 25, 1988.

I'm quite amazed at Seth's progress and interest in fourth dimensional travel. I know one day he'll become all that I am and much more. I had a dream that I believe is a breakthrough in understanding inner plane weather within the lucid dream:

In a state of deep relaxation, I saw the dream world begin to appear in front of me, and I knew I would enter the dream world very soon. Then I was standing in a big open field of deep green grass. I breathed in the sweet smell of the air.

Knowing that I was dreaming, I lifted up into the air, flying close to the clouds, feeling the thin air passing over my body. I flew faster and faster, thinking how much fun it would be to sky dive with no parachute. Looking down through scattered clouds, I could see beautiful patterns on the ground far below. Taking in a deep breath, I began to free fall, feeling my face squash against my cheekbones as I fell through the air at high speed. The ground was getting closer and closer with every second. I had to use all my power to concentrate and remember that I was dreaming in order to keep control and not wake up. The ground was approaching fast as I directed my thoughts and emotions to imagining what it would be like to float in the air. Slowly, I began to slow down and float. I landed on the ground light as a feather, my emotions calm and my mind focused.

"Jamie, stop playing around and use your lucid dreams for more important things!" I heard from my higher self.

"I'm practicing how to control my thoughts and emotions so I know how to move within the dream world and accomplish my intention," I reply.

I saw a storm building in the distance, a storm different than any storm I'd seen before. Lightening was distorting everything in its path, and the clouds seemed to be transforming everything, as if creating a new reality.

"Jamie, if you want to practice directed thinking and induced emotion, you must raise your vibratory rate and get away from this storm. Its intention is greed and selfishness, having a direct relationship to the way humans have become, and it cannot allow love to be spread throughout the universe. This powerful negative energy affects all planes of existence, including the cosmic plane where the cosmic beings exist. So, Jamie, you must not let this storm overcome you. You must wake up now." My higher self was speaking with some urgency. The storm was getting closer with every second, and I was very confused. Trying to focus on what I'd just heard

from my higher self, I remembered how all things are connected to a cosmic world with cosmic beings, and humans are like the cells of the body within the cosmic being. Using the power of directed thinking and induced emotion, I created energy around me that is reflected by the Moon. I began to feel sweet nurturing love flow through my body, as if I was in my mother's loving arms.

The storm hit me with all its angry power, but I managed to keep concentrating on the Moon and its nurturing energy, projecting images of life's nurturing power. I felt the storm's anger building into rage as its full force reached me. I continued to focus on feelings of love and nurturing, and then I also concentrated on the spiritual power of universal welfare. My attention was focused on both individual and universal love and nurturing. I got images of the whole process of life, seeing everything and everyone working within a universal plan to nurture each other in a complex, never ending cycle of life and evolution.

The storm began to break up around me. As the lightening stopped and the clouds evaporated, I found myself surrounded by beings of golden light. I felt every part of them as their rays of spiritual light danced all around and through me.

Bathed in the golden beings of loving light, I knew I had succeeded in using the power of directed thinking and induced emotion to raise my vibratory state enough to transform my character in a situation that was discordant. This was part of the path of a spiritual alchemist where he transforms his entire character in order to express tranquility and beauty radiating with spirituality.

But the storm was powerful enough to leave the residue of its energy all around me, making me feel very sick.

I decided to wake up by will, and with that thought I watched as the dream world slowly faded, then disappeared, and the material plane appeared as I woke up in my bed.

I stop reading, amazed at the description of my father's lucid dream, and suddenly realize what kind of situation I was in during the encounter with the storm in my last lucid dream. Looking back at the entry in the diary, I see a small explanation of my father's dream experience:

Explanation: After having this lucid dream, I knew what the spiritual alchemists were really trying to transform and why. There is a cosmic plane that is a counterpart to everything. The vast lack of love on the earth has caused a great sickness to spread throughout all planes of existence, and my son Seth is somehow an integral part of a great cosmic plan.

"Seth, do you understand how important it is to master the art of direct thinking and induced emotion?" I hear form my higher self.

"I'm trying to understand," I say, puzzled and confused. I need to know more what other experiences my father had with the golden city of light. Also, why did he think I'd be a part of a cosmic plan?

Somehow I know that the powerful storm I encountered in my last lucid dream was a sickness that is spreading throughout the world, and that the dream world and the waking world are the same thing.

"You're beginning to understand," my higher self says softly. I quickly pull out my tape recorder to jot down my thoughts.

Recording January 2, 1999, 8:50 a.m.

I now understand that the dream world and the waking world are the same. And it just occurred to me that everything that moves faster than the speed of light is part of the dream world, and everything that moves slower than the speed of light is part of the waking world. Our thoughts and emotions create what exists in the dream world.

IMPORTANT NOTE: If the dream world is the place of our thoughts and emotions, then the dream world creates the waking world for us to perceive, and spiritual alchemy is the key to attaining control and awareness while dreaming or while awake.

I close my stop recording with a clearer understanding of what my journey is about and why spiritual alchemists sought so desperately to transform their characters. I'm beginning to realize that I'm a spiritual alchemist and that I have an important journey ahead of me.

The next entry in my father's diary that has Amber in it is titled "Lucid dreaming by pneumonic induction".

March 6, 1989

As I watched the ocean waves crash onto the beach, I noticed that a series of spirals formed as the water washed across the sand back into the sea. I thought of how important the spiral is to all life and how all things make a spiral toward spirituality. Everything around me was very vivid, but I had no clue how I got to this shore.

Then I realized that I was dreaming. Looking at my hands, and flipping them back and forth, reassured me that I was in a dream. I remembered my intention to find Amber and the Golden City.

I shifted my attention away from the waves on the shore and focused on my intention. I lifted up into the air and hovered above the water, feeling the excitement of flying move quickly though my body. I was very strongly aware of the dream world, and felt the most control I had in a long time.

I imagined what the Golden City looked and felt like, and in the next moment the city of golden light appeared in front of me, more beautiful than the last time I saw it. The walls of the city were made of light glowing like huge crystals in the sun, and the city's energy radiated like the sun heating the earth. I focused my attention on the beautiful city and flew slowly toward it.

"Jamie, if you want to go into the city you must sustain the vibration of universal welfare. Think 'love'," I heard from my higher self.

I focused all my concentration on pure love, and flew through one of the glowing walls of the city. A powerful euphoria flowed through my body and into my soul as I entered the city. Love was very strong all around me, and I understood that if I wanted to stay in the city I had to sustain the emotion of pure love.

Holding the feelings of pure love and universal welfare, I entered a beautiful building, and went into large room where beings of pure light, with wingspans of at least ten feet, were everywhere. Amazed, I watched as hundreds of these light beings flew through the air, spreading colored light throughout the room. Rainbow colors flowed all around, covering everything with spiritual love and happiness.

The light beings saw me and flew toward me, swirling around me and radiating light with their every movement. They were trying to do something that I seemed to be a part of. Then a big flash of purple light struck me, covering my body with light, spreading a beautiful aura through my body and radiating outward, mixing with the colors around me.

I suddenly understood that the light beings created the Golden City, and their purpose was part of the cosmic plan of good. They are key to the planets' seasonal cycle in the universe, manifesting as summer, winter, spring and fall, and all working together to create progression on earth.

Looking into the distance, I saw a beautiful woman moving toward me. There was a glow around her body, and her eyes sparkled like twinkling stars.

"Jamie, Seth is coming," she said in a tranquil voice that instantly calmed me.

"Who is Seth?" I asked

The woman slowly lifted her hands, palms up, and a glowing ball of translucent light appeared in her hands. As the ball grew bigger and bigger, I could see a faint image of a young man inside the sphere.

He was sitting in my house, reading my diary.

I almost drop my father's diary, shaken and amazed at what I'm reading. Why hadn't my father told me about these experiences?

"Keep reading and be strong, Seth," my higher self says in a soft and gentle voice in my mind.

Very puzzled and very curious, I look down at diary in my hand, and continue to read.

The young man reading my diary looked familiar. "Jamie, this young man is your son Seth," the beautiful woman said.

"My son? How can that be? Who are you?"

"My name is Amber. Your son Seth is more important than you can imagine. He'll grow to develop his natural abilities and go on a wonderful journey to become a pure spiritual being. He'll spread magic throughout the universe."

"How do you know this, Amber?"

"I'm Seth's counterpart, and one day he and I will unite to create a beautiful and powerful angel. It's up to you to help him become interested in the process of alchemy and lucid dreaming so that he can purify his character and raise his vibration high enough to contact this Golden City. When that happens, we'll unite and our great work will begin.

"Jamie, wake up now by will so that you won't forget any detail of what I just told you about Seth and his journey. You must write it down in your diary."

Then Amber disappeared, leaving me immersed in the beauty and love that filled the Golden City.

"Jamie, it's time to wake up now and write down what Amber told you," my higher self says.

I imagine what it's like to be in my bed. I slowly spin around in a clockwise motion, repeating over and over, "I will wake up and remember all that I have experienced."

I lower the diary and close my eyes. I'm a sense of responsibility that I never thought I would have, knowing that I'm a big piece to a puzzle created by angels. Amazed at my father's dream experience, I lean my head back, feeling many emotions.

Anxiously, I read the next paragraph in my father's diary. It's a note to me from him.

Seth, I know that one day you'll read this. When you do, remember that I love you. Your journey and this work with the angels are no joking matter.

It's work of the greatest importance to all life.

Tears fill my eyes. I put my father's diary on the bed and close my eyes. I miss him so very much, and wonder how I can go on this chosen journey without his guidance.

"Please don't worry, Seth. This is a very important journey, but you have me as your guide, and I'll never let you down," my higher self says with sincerity.

"How can I go on this journey when I feel so alone and miss my father so much? I need his guidance," I say, angrily throwing his diary across the room.

"As you begin the purification process and realize where you are right now, your character will begin to transform, your senses will become enhanced, and you'll understand that you're not alone. You'll understand that you have a lot of support and love around you. Hang in there, have faith, and remember that you are not alone. You must trust that."

Chapter 3
The awakening

CHAPTER 3

THE AWAKENING

I slowly step into the salt solution water of the isolation floatation tank, feeling the warmth seep into my body. In this new tank I almost always enter the lucid dream state. The surrounding silent darkness feels like I'm floating in endless, open space. I begin my meditation, thinking only of love and beauty. I must raise my vibration level to a point of spiritual love if I'm going to find Amber and the Golden City. I see a faint light and hear beautiful musical chimes in the distance.

A buzzing vibrates through my body as a huge tunnel appears in front of me.

The faint light becomes a beam of light on my face.

"Seth, keep your intentions one with the feeling of love so you don't wake up." The words of my guide echo through me, soft but insistent.

The buzzing vibration grows stronger in my body, and in the next moment my journey begins.

With a strong pulling sensation, I fall into the tunnel, then fly out the other side into a blinding array of colors. As my eyes adjust to hundreds of colors flashing everywhere, I see stars and fractals all around me, like a giant kaleidoscope encompassing my soul.

"Concentrate, Seth, or you'll wake up! Don't think. Feel what's happening around you. Feel from your heart," my guide insists.

Keeping in mind the words of my guide, I look down to my left and see something deep within this world of flashing colored energy.

Eyes. Are those eyes? Yes. They're the eyes of an old man crouching in the distance, blending like a chameleon with the surrounding colored light.

All of a sudden the shadow of giant wings spreads across my body. I look up to see a being with a head pointed in the back and curved like a bird in the front. As it glides over me I realize that I'm not alone in this world of electric colors. I watch the winged being fly away and disappear into the colored light.

What was that? Should I be frightened? Excited?

"You must keep your thoughts separate from your feelings if you're going to accomplish your intention." Right. My intention. I'm grateful to my guide for that reminder, and focus my complete attention on the Golden City and Amber, filling my entire being with love.

The old man is flying toward me. his appearance creates a contrast to the surrounding colored light, like night and day mixed together in the same moment. I remember my life back on earth and become fully lucid in this dream, knowing that I'm in the floatation tank within the spiritual plane.

"Concentrate! This could be it. This could be who you have been waiting for!"

I gather all my courage, not knowing what might happen. The man, old in appearance but young in feeling, is now standing right in front of me, one hand raised in greeting, palm facing toward me, and the other hand pointing in my direction. I'm confused, but drawn toward him. Without thinking, I put my right hand on top of his.

With that movement I find myself being pulled higher up into the air. I look down and see flashing colored light shooting into the bottom and out the top of giant pillars, creating the electric world around me. I watch in wonder as thousands of winged beings of light, like the one that flew over me a moment ago, crouch and spread their wings, dispersing into the colored light. They're pulled into the pillars, and then fly out the other end, over and over in an endless cycle of beautiful, blending colored light.

Who are these beings? What are they doing? Where am I?

I'm confused and in complete bliss at the same time. "Seth, remember your intention!" my guide exclaims.

Right. My intention. I must concentrate! I think of Amber and the Golden City that my father had encountered in his explorations.

The man whose hand I touched is gone. Once again, I'm alone in an unfamiliar place, not knowing what to do. Suddenly, my hands are flashing like the colored lights that surround me. Then the colors begin to fade as a dark fog descends over everything. Loneliness fills my soul and cold chills run up and down my body. I can think of only one thing - I am alone forever. A feeling of deep emptiness begins to grow in the center of my stomach, and the beauty that encircled me a moment ago has faded to a dark cold fog. The beautiful winged beings of wonder and spirituality are nowhere to be found.

"Wake up now, Seth, and prepare for what's going to come," my guide says, worried.

What about my intention? What about Amber and the Golden City? I think I'm very close now."

"Forget about that right now and wake up! Something is happening. Something . . . "the voice fades.

"Where are you going? Are you there?" I call out. Fear creeps inside me. "Where are you?" I scream.

I close my eyes and think of the isolation floatation tank and my life back on earth. I feel the warm salt water around my body, and start to wake up. I think it's very strange that my guide would just disappear like that. Why?

I climb out of the tank, salt on my skin, water dripping onto the floor. It's all so dream-like.

Every time I get out of the floatation tank, I feel like I'm in a dream even though I'm awake. I wait for my senses to come back, then grab my tape recorder and record the whole experience, still wondering why my guide disappeared like that. What could have such an impact on the connection I have with my higher self while in the dream state?

A warm shower leaves my skin soft and healthy from the minerals in the Epson salts that keep me afloat in the tank, but emotionally I feel very alone and confused. I've always believed that our guides, or our intuition or higher selves, are with us at all times, and would never leave us, especially in circumstances like the one I just experienced.

But my guide, who has helped me in so many situations over the years, has left me. What will I do without him? Loneliness overwhelms me. I slump to the bathroom floor and start to cry. Tears roll down my face and fall to my feet, splashing and bursting into tiny drops. Why must I be so alone? Why?

Finally, emotionally exhausted, I get up off the floor and walk to my bedroom. My father's diary is on my bed, and I feel some comfort knowing that even if I'm alone I still have it to guide me when I need help.

I anxiously search the diary's index for something that could explain why and where my guide could have gone. Then I see an index titled "Vibratory rate: Staying in tune with your guides. pp 72." I rush through the pages in desperate anticipation.

November 25, 1997.

I have now developed my skill to the point where I can enter the lucid dream by will. My experiences have continued to give me a more significant understanding of the process of spiritual transformation. I've had many experiences lately that relate to Seth and his importance to this work, but after my last visit with Amber, I can't say anything to Seth about his role in the cosmic plan. I must choose what I tell him carefully and wisely, because of my influence on his development. Too much information too soon will definitely alter his natural evolutionary path.

I put the diary down, wondering what my father could have told me that would alter my life. I notice places in the diary where pages have been torn out. I'll have to wait until I can learn about this mystery from direct experience. I try to remember everything about lucid dreaming my father told me when he was alive, but can't think of anything that could be so important. Frustrated and discouraged, I don't even want to think about trying to find my guide. Instead, I start to cry again. I pick the diary up again and continue reading as I wipe tears from my face.

Moving swiftly into the dream state, my guide gave me the cue: "Jamie, you're dreaming. I want to show you something very important."

"What could be more important than this?" I thought as I gazed in wonder at the Golden City, its illuminating beauty soaking through me to my soul. Every time I'm in this city I feel only love and happiness.

"That's what I wanted to show you, Jamie; how to feel love and happiness. What happens in the dream world when you're feeling love? What happens when you're not feeling love? Our emotions determine our experience in the dream world. Your unique ability to feel love and happiness causes you to experience this place of beauty."

"You mean the Golden City wouldn't exist if I didn't feel love? I didn't know that I was powerful enough to create such a place."

"No, Jamie. The Golden City exists because many people and beings are feeling love, and you're seeing and experiencing it because you feel love as they do. Love raises your vibration so you can travel to a different level of the dream world. Love gives you the ability to see and experience things like the Golden City."

"So if I felt sad or angry right now within this lucid dream, would everything change?"

"That's right. You don't change the things around you, but when your mood changes, things that have a similar vibration to your emotions are attracted to you. You literally travel in the dream state with your emotions.

"Do you mean that if I want to travel the different planes of existence in the dream world, all I have to do is change my mood?"

"Exactly. But you must be careful. If you change your mood to anything evil, you'll find yourself in an environment that's of the same vibration, and it's very difficult to change it back because all the things around you will have the same evil intentions."

"But all I have to do is wake up if it gets too strange for me, right?

"Right. You'll wake up from the dream, but your emotions will still be the same as in the dream. It's important to remember that your mood, your emotions, your feelings, whatever you want to call them, determine what place you find yourself in the dream world, whether awake or dreaming. The only difference is that when you're dreaming you experience the environment that you're feeling, and when you're awake you

consciously feel it as you experience the environment that you've created. But whether dreaming or awake, the experience affects you the same way."

"How does it affect me the same whether I'm awake or dreaming?"

"Every thought and feeling of love, pure joy, or universal welfare causes you to raise your dominant vibration. Every thought and feeling of hate, anger or fear causes you to lower your dominant vibration. This is the essence of evolution. And it's possible, when you reach a point where you can sustain the experiences of love long enough, and keep your dominant vibration raised high enough, to transform into an angel."

An angel. That's what my father told me the night before he died. I hear him again, as if he was right next to me, "Seth, that's what this is all about - angels!" I read on, trying to figure out what this has to do with finding my guide.

"Jamie, you need to know one more thing that's very important. If your vibration is too low, you'll lose contact with me."

"What? How can that be possible? You're always with me, even when I'm awake!"

"I'm always with you because you're usually feeling love, but if you start to have negative feelings, you'll lower your vibration to a level where I'm not able to go. You see, Jamie, I'm your higher self, not your lower self. I'm the love and spiritual part of you that's always looking out for your best interests. But I can't travel though the different planes of the dream world as you can, and if you get out of my vibration, I'll disappear and won't be there to help you."

"I think I want to see that for myself. I need to understand what you're talking about."

"Ok, but be very careful. If you go too far into a negative place, you may have a hard time coming back and depression may set in."

"You mean I could get stuck there?"

"Yes, you could, and I wouldn't be able to help you feel love again until you get out of the depression and start feeling love."

The next pages were torn out of the diary, as if my father didn't want anyone to read about his experience of lowering his vibration.

A thought comes to me as I close the diary. All I have to do is feel love rather than sadness and my guide will come back! My deep loneliness must have lowered my vibration and made my guide disappear, and I've been depressed and alone since then. Curious to see what my father experienced when he went to a lower vibrational level in the dream state, I decide to go into the isolation floatation tank, get lucid, and experience this in the dream world.

It was strange to be in the tank without my guide to start me on my journey into the lucid dream. He's usually right with me, helping me with every step of entering the dream.

Surrounded by almost total darkness, I start to relax and focus my attention on my third eye. I visualize my hands in front of me, flipping them over with each breath and each count. "One I'm dreaming, two I'm dreaming, three I'm dreaming, four I'm dreaming, . . ."

At eighty-five, a bright light appears from behind my head and moves to stop in front of my face. I know that I'm in the dream state. I see my thoughts coming out of my head and floating in front of me, a definite sign that I'm dreaming.

Then I'm standing on a cliff so high that when I look down, I can't see the ground at the bottom. My hand is in front of me as though I'm about to take off flying, then I'm in the air and the wind is gently passing over my body. I know I'm dreaming and flying though the air in my dream. I'm exhilarated as the lucidity gets stronger with every moment. My intention. I must find my guide.

I land in a beautiful, open field, and sit cross-legged in the soft, green grass. Closing my eyes, I start to meditate in my dream, breathing deeply and thinking only of love.

I reach an altered state within this dream world as I find myself standing in the open field, looking at myself sitting in the open field. I'm aware that I'm meditating in the dream, and I'm aware that I'm out of my body standing next to myself as I meditate. I look so peaceful sitting there with my eyes closed, and I feel peaceful as I remember how wonderful it is to dream again.

I raise my hands up so that my palms are facing each other, and begin to build up loving energy between my hands. I place my glowing hands on the shoulders of my sitting body and pass loving energy through myself, feeling extreme happiness and joy. I think, "This is incredible! I'm passing energy though my body that's sitting in meditation, and I can feel that energy in this body that I'm in right now!"

My vision starts to fill with light as everything around me begins to fade. My sitting self, the mountains in the background and the beautiful field of grass, all look transparent, like I'm in two places at once. My mind is filled with inspiration, love fills my heart, and aspiration flows into my being.

Everything around me fades away, and suddenly I'm surrounded by the flashing colored light and the crouching winged beings. Crouching and spreading, crouching and spreading, the beings are in an endless dance of creation.

"Seth, you made it!" I hear my guide's voice.

"Is that really you?" I ask, astonished and relieved.

"Yes, it's me. Your guide is back. Or rather, you're back!" "That was a wonderful experience until I thought of my father and began to feel so lonely. The next thing I knew, you were gone!"

"Can you understand now that love is the only thing that can keep us together? If you persist on feeling alone and empty, then we'll lose each other. I'm amazed at how you were able to find me. You have a gift, Seth. You have the ability to travel through planes of the dream world. Do you know what that means?"

"No. And what do you mean we'll lose each other? How can I lose a part of myself?"

"You humans get so attached to a certain idea or feeling that you become obsessed with it, creating a pattern of emotions that are sustained by your thoughts. That pattern then creates your perception of looking at things, and this perception becomes a reality to you, attracting circumstances that feed your pattern. This has become an endless cycle with humans that are very difficult to break. But you have a gift that you cannot take for granted. Learn how to develop it so you can find your father and your counterpart, so you can let go once and for all."

"Is my father still alive?"

"We're always alive. When one part of us dies, another part of us is reborn. That's why it's so important to stop perpetuating as many patterns as possible before that time comes, because when you pass on, the patterns remain with you. These patterns hinder our evolution and our ability to become an angel."

"Where is my father? Is he an angel?" I ask, remembering to keep feeling love and happiness while thinking of my father, knowing that I could lose my guide if I'm not careful.

"No, he's not an angel. Seth, I'm going to tell you something, and I don't want you to get upset."

"What could be more upsetting then the fact that my father is gone?" I say with some emotion.

"That's just it. He's not gone. He lives in the dream world.

He's stuck in one of his patterns."

"Is he stuck in the dream world?"

"Your father was carrying a lot of guilt about certain things he did before you were born. He never settled those things, choosing to ignore them while on earth. When he passed away, he still had these patterns to deal with, and he became stuck in a world of guilt, a sort of dream hell."

"Is there really such a place as hell?"

"We each create our own hell by staying in our perceived reality of our patterns. It's a very tricky place to be in because you've created it yourself, and you're stuck there until you wake up and confront the pattern. Most of the people back on earth live their lives stuck in their patterns, believing it's the only reality. Seth, you have to go and get your father out of his hell so you can let go of

him and transform into what you came here to be."

"Get my father out of hell?"

"Show him that he's replaying a pattern of the past so that he can continue on his path. But you must not get stuck in his world. You must not let his emotions affect your intention or you may find yourself in trouble there. You have the gift to carry you through your journey, starting with this one. And there will be many more to come."

"How will I find him? How will I know what to do when I find him?"

"In your father's room there's a secret compartment behind the picture of your mother that hangs on the wall. The answer to your questions are there."

A dark cloud is building in the distance. Lightning crashes out of it in all directions as the cloud grows bigger and bigger. This swirling mass of blackness is sucking up everything in its path, including the wonderful winged beings and the flashing electrical environment they were creating.

"Is that another storm?" I ask.

"Yes, Seth, it is. But this storm will not pass. It'll continue to destroy everything in its path."

"Why?"

"Let me explain. Right now you and the entire universe are going through a very powerful transformation. Positive, spiritual energy and negative, non-spiritual energy are mixing together. This storm is powerful negative energy, spreading evil and hatred like a disease, destroying everything it comes in contact with. But, as you transform, you'll help counter this non-spiritual energy with loving, spiritual energy, and put the cosmic plane and back on its path. This transformation will be the beginning of the unity of all planes of existence. These planes will gather together for a short time, then separate."

"What will happen then? Will everything change?" "Indeed it will! Our entire universe, physical and non-physical, is a cosmic being with its own evolution and progression. This cosmic being is ready to transform, like a caterpillar that's ready to transform into a butterfly. But the negative energy that's spreading throughout the world has weakened the cosmic being and made it very sick, preventing its transformation."

"What will happen to the earth? What will happen to us?" I'm very worried.

"The planets are aligning to create a shift of the earth's electric and magnetic poles. During this shift, the cosmic being will assimilate all its knowledge and combine all parts of itself, and time will stand still in the earth realm for three days. One part of the world will experience a long day, and the opposite side of the world will experience a long night. In the dream world, the destructive force that you see now as a storm and spiritual light will mix together, creating confusion in both the physical and non-physical worlds. All beings, no matter how small or large, simple or complex, will be attracted to the place that's exactly the same as the energy they have inside. The dream world will split into seven different worlds of progression and vibratory states. The world of lowest vibratory rate will express only hell and devils (pure evil), the next world will have a higher vibratory rate, and the next will have a still higher vibration, until, at the seventh world, only heaven and angles (pure love) exist. Each of us will go to the world that reflects our energy."

"Will the earth survive this transformation?"

"The earth will transform as well. During the three day shift, distance will disappear, gravity will be lost, and all beings will instantly be attracted to one of the seven separate dream worlds, depending on the quality of their character. When the cosmic being has completed its transformation, distance and gravity will return to the earth, and all beings will awaken in the earth plane. There will be changes, but no one, not even the most intelligent guide, knows what those changes will be. The earth is a mixture of all planes expressing as one, and when the cosmic being is finished with its transformation, what the earth will be like will depend on what the cosmic being becomes next."

I feel a cold wind, and look up and to see that the black storm is very close. Fear grips me as if I'm being chased by something from which there is no escape.

"Seth, remember, wherever you go, you are there. There is no escape from yourself," my guide says, his voice fading as if it was being sucked up by the storm.

Surrounded by blackness, I seem to be planted on the last piece of spirituality. I draw up all my courage and use the power of my mind to keep my emotions in a place of love and universal welfare. As the storm crushes me with surges of fear, I jump into the center the blackness, diving into a black hole that seems to swirl into infinity.

Then I'm feeling the warm salt water of the floatation tank, and I'm awake. The swirling storm fades into the blackness of the tank. I open the tank's door to let my eyes adjust to the light. When I close my eyes against the light, my whole experience flashes in front of me in an instant, reminding me of the cosmic being and the secret hiding place.

I climb out of the tank, feeling a bit dizzy, and wonder if I'm still dreaming. Drops of water fall off of my body, just like the last time I got out of the tank and had my shower, but these drops fall in slow motion, taking forever to hit the floor, and when they do, they splash and break into hundreds of tiny drops. I close my eyes and think "Is this a dream, or am I awake?"

I open my eyes and pick up a piece of paper on my desk. It's a note that I had written to myself. I look at the note, look away for a moment, and then look back. The writing doesn't change, so I must be awake. If I was dreaming, the writing would have changed.

"What's going on?" I ask my guide.

No response.

"Are you there?" I yell out loud.

Silence. Did I lose my guide again? I dry myself off and go into my father's old room, where I see the picture of my mother on the wall. Feeling lonely again, I lift the picture off its hook, and sure enough, there's a small compartment with a gold box inside. I'm so curious about the box that I completely forget that my guide isn't with me.

I take the box out of the compartment and put it on the bed. On the front is a picture of a man standing with his arms and legs spread out, inside of two triangles, one right side up and the other upside-down. A circle is drawn around the triangles. Everything in the picture is geometrically proportioned with all the angles and spaced exactly the same. A ball of light is drawn on the man's chest, at the solar plexus level.

The image looks very old, but it makes me feel very powerful. I know that it has something to do with what I'm going to find inside. As I open the box, it feels like magic is in the air, like I'm in a dream. Inside the box, on the right side, is a note marked "Seth". It says:

> ***Dear Seth,***
>
> ***If you're reading this letter, I guess you're on your way to finding me. I want you to be very careful. This is not a game, and you must take everything that you do from this point on very seriously.***
>
> ***I love you a lot.***
>
> ***What you're going to experience next may be a bit strange. Just remember that no matter how much your waking reality feels like a dream, you still have to obey the rules of nature and gravity. No jumping from any cliffs or buildings like we do in the dream world!***
>
> ***Seth, your guide is not with you because you're supposed to do this by yourself. Your guide does not have the ability to help you where you are going next.***
>
> ***This letter is the only guidance you'll be getting, so pay very close attention to the words that are written next.***

I set the letter down for a moment, feeling as if my father is right next to me, speaking these words. A soothing sensation comes over me as I pick up the letter to see what's next.

Seth, no matter where you are, no matter what plane of existence you travel to, there's one thing that's always the same: You. That's right. You are always you no matter where you go, and it's important to remember that as you continue.

Do you know what the Merkaba is? The picture that you saw on the front of the gold box represents the Merkaba, which is the energy field each one of us has. This energy field spreads twenty feet in all directions around your body. When you get your Merkaba spinning in the right way, the waking world becomes a dream and you can travel to any place or dimension you wish.

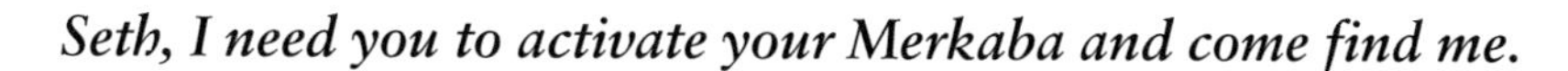

Seth, I need you to activate your Merkaba and come find me.

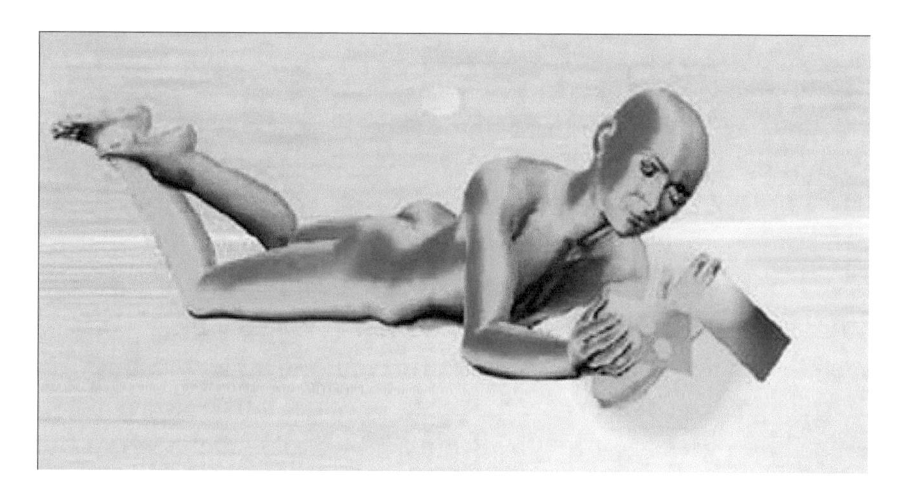

In the box there are three crystal balls that I found long before you were born. As long as you have the feeling of love coming from inside of you, these crystal balls have the power to activate your Merkaba by using the electromagnetic energy coming from your body to power them.

The crystals can do many things depending on the amount of love you are feeling. Their power will be very strong in your hands if you can illuminate the feeling of love for all beings in the universe that have guided you since you were born.

When you use the crystals a lot, the dream world and waking world will become one, and things may seem a bit strange. So always remember to test your state of consciousness. I' hate to see you do something foolish if you thought that you were dreaming when you are really awake!

You have the power to become lucid at any given moment, and as you develop your ability to feel more love, you will activate your Merkaba. That's when you'll be able to come for me.

Remember, Seth: goodness alone is power.

Love,
Jamie

I put the letter down and look at the front of the box. How did my father know that I was going to get him, and where is he? How will I know where to go to find him?

Inside the gold box are three small crystal balls about the size of marbles. They illuminate a green glow. I pick one up and instantly feel a warmth in my heart that soothes my entire body. When I pick up the second one, the warmth moves into my stomach and solar plexus. My hand feels warm as I reach for the third glowing crystal. As the three crystal balls touch each other in the palm of my right hand, the warmth and feeling of love spread throughout my entire body, filling me with joy and laughter. A greenish golden color begins to spread over my hand, slowly moving up my arm. In minutes I'm surrounded by a green golden glow from head to toe. I feel power as a tingling sensation on every inch of my body. It's ecstasy!

I sit cross-legged and begin to breathe in the golden light of the crystal balls. I feel it filling my body with warmth and lighting my soul. It's as if I'm breathing a soothing, warm fog that goes into my nose and swirls down my spine reaching my toes. With every breath the sensations become stronger and more powerful. I close my eyes, and a yellow golden energy fills my vision, sparkling in my head. Swirling around and around, the golden light gives shape as time and gravity disappear.

I think, "I'm dreaming. I can feel it. I'm dreaming."

My father's room quickly fades, and I find myself-floating in the clouds, staring out into the distance.

There it is, the beautiful Golden City. With two angles guarding the front gate. Temples built of gold and bigger than any sky-scraper in any city on earth, glow in the sun. Silvery, white, luminous light surrounds the city like a dome, spreading light all around like the sun shimmering its beauty as it rises over a clear ocean.

"So you found the box I was talking about," I hear my guide say.

"Is that you, my wonderful companion?"

"Yes, Seth, and I'm amazed at your ability to feel love. I thought it would take you at least a week to get to the Golden City, but you did it without even trying. Come, let's go."

"Where are we going?"

"Don't you want to see the inside of the city?" "Oh, yes! I'd love the see what's on the inside!"

"Well, come on. You remember how to fly, don't you?" Feeling a bit overwhelmed with having to continue illuminating love, I lift up into the air and slowly fly toward the Golden City, trying to remember all the times I had flown in my other lucid dream experiences.

"Come on, Seth, let's go!" my guide urges me on.

A shimmering figure appears next to me. It looks a shadow made of sparkling light. It starts to fly toward the city.

"What are you waiting for? Let's get going!" my guide says as he flies faster.

Excited, I follow my guide, flying right behind him. "Is that as fast as you can go?" I say, joking a bit.

A flash of light comes from behind the shadowy figure, and in an instant it zooms about a hundred feet in front of me.

"You think you're so experienced, well then try that my golden boy!"

Using all the concentration I have, I think of moving faster, like a rocket blasting into space. Boy, am I moving fast! I can feel my cheeks splatter on my face as I pick up speed. But it's not even close to what my guide has just done.

"Not bad, Seth, but if you must stop using concepts from earth to gather your speed in this place, you'll move faster than the speed of light. Any time you use a thought and an emotion from earth, like a rocket going into space, you may think you're going faster, but what you're really doing is slowing yourself down!"

Pondering that for a moment, I realize that he's talking about using the thought of teleportation to move quickly. As I think of teleportation, in an instant I'm right next to my guide. We're right in front of the Golden City.

The beautiful city seems to go on forever, disappearing into the clouds and into nothing but light.

"I guess you've never seen anything like this big before," my guide says.

"You're right. This tops them all!"

"Wait until you see what's on the inside. All the beautiful things you could possibly imagine are there, including the angels."

"Angels? I thought that the crouching beings were angels." "Oh, no. As spectacular as the crouching beings are, they're nothing compared to the angelic form. Seth, it's very important for you to understand that within the Golden City everything is very different than anything you now know, and it will change you." My guide grows suddenly serious.

"What do you mean 'different'? How will I be changed?" "First, you must remember that when you want to go somewhere in the Golden City, you must think of doing something for someone or something else. Just thinking about going somewhere won't work. You must think about taking someone else, and then you'll go there. Also, the city may look big from the outside, but when you get inside you'll know that there is no size to pure spirituality. It is infinite. There may seem to be walls on the outside of the city, but when you get inside, all of that will change."

"Ok, ok. Let's go!" I say, eager to see the inside of this marvelous city, and trying to sound like I'm prepared for this experience when I'm really feeling a bit intimidated by everything my guide is telling me.

"Don't worry, Seth. Just remember to keep feeling the love, then direct it toward someone or something, and you'll do fine," says my guide with encouragement.

"Ok, I'm ready."

The wall in front of us begins to look like water with a silvery glow to it. What appears to be solid is now a soft clear liquid waving like a flag in the wind. I can see my reflection in it.

"Just walk right through it, Seth."

I reach out to touch the silvery liquid and my hand goes right through it. As I walk through the Golden City wall, I'm struck by a feeling I never felt before awaking every part of my being.

Chapter 4

The confusion

CHAPTER 4

THE CONFUSION

"Seth, remember that you can't think of yourself when you're in the Golden City. Everything you do must be an act of kindness for something or someone else."

Suddenly, I'm having the strongest feelings of inspiration and aspiration that I've ever had. But, to my amazement, I also feel very helpless.I see something flying toward me, but I can't make out what it is. A gentle breeze brushes through my hair as it passes over me. My eyes begin to adjust to the light that fills the Golden City, and there in the distance, flying with complete grace though the air, are winged beings with tails like dolphins.

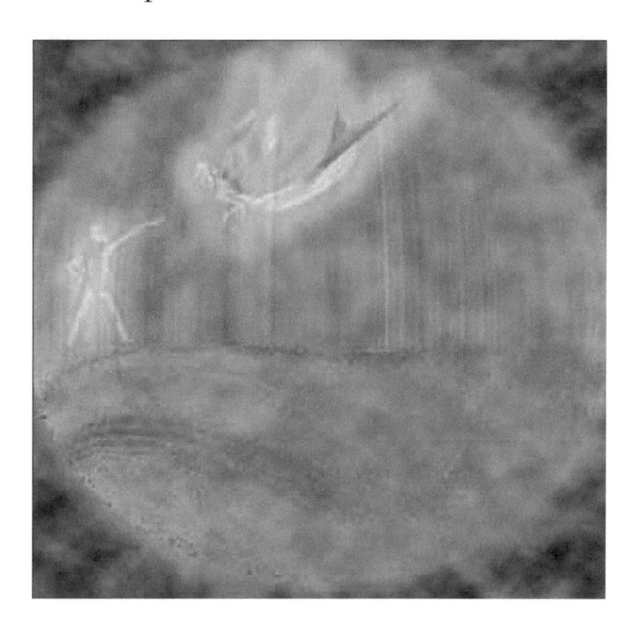

Gracefully swaying back and forth, thrusting themselves forward with every movement, they glide through the light reflecting off their bodies. Long, thin arms stretch out over their heads. Their fingers glow and sparkle, almost blending into the surrounding light. Twenty feet long translucent wings stretch out from either side of their magnificently shaped bodies, moving up and down like the wings of giant birds. They're flying into the sun as it sets over the ocean. One winged being passes directly over me and I see that its head is very similar in shape to a human head, but with features that are neither male nor female. Its eyes are a brightly glowing greenish color, and they seem to pierce my soul as it looks directly at me, and then flies passed.

My eyes are fully adjusted now, and I can see everything inside the Golden City. Dozens of huge waterfalls made of a mixture of light and a silvery luminous liquid, are shining and flowing all around the city, producing a mist that fills the air and creates electrical rainbow colors that flash star-like patterns everywhere.

In the distance I see the crouching beings that I encountered before. They're performing their dance of creation in absolute harmony with the winged beings, flowing together, their energies mixing and producing a light purple aura that flows up into the sky. The purple light forms clouds that are alive and moving, making pictures of nature: an ocean with the sun setting, mountains with and without snow, forests with swaying trees, and deep green jungles.

Beautiful music fills the air and everything is moving in the same rhythm, like in an animated musical, all in complete harmony, dancing the dance of true spiritual creation.

I'm filled with love and joy. I start to fly in the direction my guide went, but I can't move at all! I concentrate on moving, but nothing happens.

"Use the feeling of universal welfare. Feel like you're doing something for someone else and don't expect to get anything in return," my guide says, as if it were easy to do.

I realize that I'm a baby in a new world and that it'll take some time to develop my ability to function in it. I remember what my father said to me once: "No matter where you go, there you are." For the first time in my life I realize how important it is to develop the ability to give and not expect anything in return.

"Seth, it's time to go for you father."

"My father. Yes, I must go," I say, feeling confident and exited to see him again. It's been so long.

"As you travel to where your father is, it's very important to remember this place and the feelings that surround it. This will allow you to return here and to your home back on earth."

"I'll keep the image of this place in my heart and in my mind." "I can't travel with you. When you get back to earth you're going to change," my guide says in a soft voice. "How will I change?" I ask anxiously.

"You've been combining the dream world and the waking world, and now that you've experienced the Golden City, your character will begin to express more spiritually when you return home. Remember that you're in control of the dream. No matter how strange it may get, even if you think that you're awake, keep this place strong within you and the spiritual power of the Golden City will guide you to Amber."

With all the excitement and new experiences, I've completely forgotten about Amber! "What will happen when I finally meet Amber?"

"One thing at a time, Seth. For now, all I can tell you is that when you and Amber join together you'll be in love unlike any love you have ever experienced. Now go. Have a safe journey. We here in the Golden City will keep you in our thoughts."

Thousands of green glowing eyes turn to look at me, as if my journey to find my father is incredibly important to the welfare of the Golden City. The rhythm of the Golden City changes as all attention is focused on me.

I remember what my guide told me about the cosmic being and the changes that are going to happen soon. The focused attention of the winged beings and the light beings makes me feel like I have a great part in the transformation of the cosmic being.

"Go now, Seth."

I feel the loneliness that's deep within me from losing my father, but keep holding a strong and clear picture of him in my mind's eye as I say, "I will be with my father where he is. I will be with my father where he is," over and over.

Using all the power of my thoughts and emotions, I think of what it used to be like when my father embraced me as a child. I fill my mind with memories of everything about him, as if he's right next to me. As this rapport starts to build, the Golden City fades, and I'm standing in a translucent hologram of it.

A dark fog starts to encompass all the light, swallowing the Golden City.

"Don't be afraid," I hear from my guide, his voice fading with the last of the light from the Golden City.

I'm now in complete darkness. I close my eyes and continue to recite my mantra, holding my father's image strong within me. "I will be with my father where he is. I will be with my father where he is. I will be with my father where he is."

The next moment I'm in a car moving very fast down a dark, creepy road. I hold onto the handle of the car door, clenching it as tight as I can. I look to my left at the driver.

There he is! My father is driving the car!

"Dad! Is that really you? Are you really alive? "I ask in amazement.

No response.

"Dad, listen to me!" I yell as loud as I can.

Nothing. He doesn't hear me. His face is tightly serious as he focuses on the road and nothing else.

"Dad, wake up! This is a dream and you must wake up now!"

He glances to his right, looking confused. He looks right through me, loneliness in his eyes.

Tears are falling down my face. "Dad, wake up now! This is a dream. Wake up!" I'm really crying now. "Dad, remember the

Golden City? Remember Amber?"

All of a sudden a bright glow of happiness enters my father's eyes.

"Seth, is that you? What's happening? You can't be here, you're in . . ." Before he can finish, a truck comes out of nowhere and hits the passenger side of the car. I feel myself crashing through the windshield. I tumble through the air and land on the road about 100 feet away. I look to see my father pulling himself from the car.

He seems to be all right.

I stand up and realize that I feel nothing. There is no blood.

I'm all right. I run to my father, who is kneeling on the ground. His head is bleeding. Moving closer to the car, I'm startled to see myself lying on the ground with blood coming from my head. My father is crying as he kneels next to his bleeding son.

"Dad, I'm over here!" I yell, moving even closer to him. "Dad up here!" I yell even louder, right into his ear. "This is a dream. You must wake up now. This is not real. Wake up! The Golden City and Amber - you must remember. You must!" I'm crouched down right next to him.

He looks up at me and says, "Son, is that you? Where are you? I can't see you."

"Dad, I'm right next to you! We're dreaming. You must wake up!"

"Seth, is this a dream?" he asks, looking right at me.

"Yes, Dad, this is a dream and I want you to know that I'm all right. I'm not hurt. Everything is ok." I begin to think of the Golden City, pouring love into my soul.

"Seth, you're ok! I can see you!" my father says. He stands up and embraces me. I'm so relieved, feeling absolute power surround us both.

"Dad, I've been to the Golden City. It was magnificent! Here, I want you to have this." I put my hand on my father's heart, projecting feelings of the love that I felt in the Golden City. A golden glow begins to flow from my hand. The more I feel the love, the bigger the glow grows, slowly surrounding my father.

"You see, Dad, everything is ok. Don't be afraid. I'm here with you now and I'm ok." My sincerity and confidence is mixed with confusion as I stare at myself lying on the ground, bleeding severely from my head.

My father looks right at me, his eyes bulging. "Seth, you must come back to us. You must come back to your mother and me!" Confusion turns to terror as he mentions my mother. She's been dead for many years. "Dad, what are you talking about? Do you know that both you and Mom are dead?"

"Dead? No, Seth. We're alive, and we want you to come home to us. You're the one that must wake up!"

"I'll wake up if that's what you want, but if I do I know you won't be there because you're dead."

Just like the Golden City fading into total darkness, my father begins to fade.

"Seth, you must come back to us! You must wake up!" My father cries out. I hear his voice grow fainter and fainter.

Then I see my father lying in bed. He's talking with a lady who I've never seen before. I wonder where I am and what's really happening. At this point I don't know what's real and what isn't. I remember my guide telling me that when I remember where I am and allow myself to let go, I'll know what it's really happening. So I let this confusing experience continue and let go of everything I think I know. I don't interact with the experience, and focus my attention on what the lady is saying to my father.

"Jamie, wake up! Wake up!" Elizabeth, my personal nurse, says excitedly. Elizabeth has been taking care of me since the car accident.

"Jamie, you must wake up! I can't believe it but I saw you move your feet!"

I look down at my feet and move them.

Elizabeth, I can do it! I can move my feet!" With all of my concentration, I focus on my legs, and they move! Elizabeth looks at me in amazement, almost as if she's going to faint. I hadn't been able to move my legs for three years, ever since the accident.

"It's a miracle!" I yell, excitement rushing through me. "Look at that! Would you look at that!" I move my legs off the bed and put a little bit of weight on them, my entire body shaking from the effort. Three years is a long time to be paralyzed and in a wheelchair. Now, suddenly, I can move my legs!

"Jamie, I don't know how it's possible that you can move your legs, but this is truly a wonderful day!" I don't know how I would have survived without Elizabeth. She's taken care of everything for me.

"Yes, Elizabeth, it's a wonderful day! And that's not all. I've spoken with my son Seth. Yes - Seth," I say in response to Elizabeth's questioning look. "Do you remember when I told you about my isolation flotation tank and all the experiments I did with lucid dreaming?"

"Yes, I remember the lucid dreaming stuff."

"Well, I had my first lucid dream since Seth and I were in the car accident. Seth was there. But the strangest thing about it was that he thought I was dead! He had no idea that he was in a coma." "Jamie, do you think Seth has been lucid dreaming in his coma for three years and thinks he's awake?"

"Yes I do, Elizabeth. I really do." I look down at my legs. They're skinny and white. Walking would take some effort, but I know I can do it.

"Seth gave me the power to walk. He healed me." "How did he do that?"

"He put some golden energy into my heart and it surrounded my entire body. He said he had visited the Golden City. I think he got the power from there."

"What's the Golden City? "Elizabeth's asked.

"There's a lot I haven't told you or anyone about the lucid dream world and the work I was so obsessed with before the accident," I say carefully.

"Jamie, I don't know anything about a Golden City, and I don't know if I can believe all these things about Seth and lucid dreaming. I just know that you can move your legs here in this reality and that's truly a miracle. That's all I care about."

The sun just starting to come up, a perfect time to get back into a lucid dream and try to contact Seth. "Elizabeth, I'm going back to bed for a little while. Would you close the window shades, please?"

Elizabeth walks over to the window and closes the shades. "Get some sleep. When you wake up we'll go visit Seth at the hospital and see if his status has changed."

As she leaves the room, I want to immediately go to the hospital, but visiting hours aren't until 9. Anyway, I knew that I'd be with him soon. As the room darkens, I feel very confident that I'll have another lucid dream.

I lie back on my bed and close my eyes. I'm relaxed and warm, and also excited at the thought of walking again. Focusing on my third eye, I begin to move a ball of light through my body, down my right arm, thinking, "The relaxation is stronger than all the tension."

As the ball of light moves over my hand and traces my fingers, I repeat the thought again: "The relaxation is stronger than all the tension."

As the ball of light passes through my body, relaxing everything in its path, I suggest to myself again that "The relaxation is stronger than all the tension."

As the ball of light reaches my stomach, the ball starts to spin, gathering all the tensions from days past, soothing me with every movement. Again and again I suggest to myself that "The relaxation is stronger than all the tension."

As the ball of light moves over my legs and reaches my spine, I focus all my attention on my intention. The ball of light spirals slowly down my spine, moving around each vertebra as I suggest to myself that "The next time I'm dreaming, I'll remember to recognize that I'm dreaming."

As the ball of light approaches my third eye, completing its journey through my body, I become completely relaxed. I think, "The total connection of absolute relaxation is now complete, and the next time I'm dreaming, I'll allow myself to recognize that I'm dreaming."

I concentrate on visualizing my dream hand in front of me, creating a triangle between my two hands and the ball of light that still holds my concentration at my third eye. I flip my dream hand over and say, "I'm dreaming." As I flip my hand over again, keeping my focus on the ball of light that fills my head and radiates from my third eye, I say, "I'm dreaming." I continue to flip my hands over and say "I'm dreaming." at each flip, and the dream world begins to appear. I'm excited in anticipation.

Still watching form above, I see my father enter a dream state. I stay in contact with him as he comes out of his body. Then I hear my guide talking to him.

"Jamie, don't get too excited or you'll wake up."

The dream is now all around me. My body feels very light, and I realize that I'm floating over my bed. Then I'm standing next to my body, which is lying peacefully on my bed. I listen to my guide and gain control of my feelings, tying to not let my excitement overwhelm me.

"Is that you? Is it really you?" I say out loud, I haven't had any contact with my guide since the accident.

"Yes, Jamie. You've been in a state of severe depression, but not you're back."

"Can you help me find Seth?" I ask, knowing that my guide can show me how to search Seth out no matter where he is.

I yell out loud, "Dad! I'm right here!" But my father doesn't react. It's as if we're in completely different worlds, yet experiencing the same thing! All I can do is watch and listen.

"Yes, Jamie. I can help you, but there's something that you must understand about Seth."

"What must I understand?"

"Seth has gone through many changes in the past three years. He's not only seen the Golden City, he's been inside it. Do you know what this means?"

"Well, I know that he had the power to heal my legs and break my depression. I know that the only place he could get that power is from the Golden City. He was talking about it when I saw him in my last lucid dream."

"That's only part of it. Seth has contacted the light beings and the winged beings. Soon he'll meet Amber. He'll return to the Golden City like before, and it'll unite him with love so that he can travel and find his great work."

"You say that as if he's not going to come home to me." "What really is 'home', Jamie?"

I'm very confused. I look at my body sleeping in my bed and think that my home is where my body is. But I know that home is where my soul is.

"That's right, Jamie. Home is where your soul is, and eventually we all end up back home."

"Are you saying that Seth won't be coming home to me? That he'll be going to do his great work in the Golden City with Amber?"

"Jamie, let's go into the other room and ask him what he wants to do. After all, the choice is ultimately up to him."

"Seth is in the other room?" I ask in disbelief. My excitement turns to fear of losing my son forever.

"Yes. He's been here all along, exploring the world that you can't see while awake."

My father turns his head in my direction, as if he's looking directly at me.

The next moment, I'm back in my father's room, holding the crystal balls that allowed me to enter the dream state. I'm so confused and scared that I start to cry. I look up, and there's my father walking toward the partly open door!

"Seth, can you hear me?" he says as he pushes the door open all the way. He looks in my direction, his eyes getting wide, just like when he used to look at me when I was a baby.

"Dad! You're here! Are you really alive or are we still dreaming? Seth asks anxiously. He takes a state test to check if he's dreaming or not, then rushes over to me and takes me into his arms, letting me know that everything's ok.

"Dad, how can you be alive? How can this be possible?" I'm so glad to see him.

"Seth, you're dreaming."

"No. This is real. I just took a state test and I know that I'm awake." I put down the crystal balls, trying to understand what's happening. I know I'm awake, but my father is standing right in front of me!

"Dad, what's going on? How can I be awake and dreaming at the same time? How can you be here?"

"Seth, what I'm going to explain to you may come as a big surprise, and I want you to stay calm."

Suddenly I notice that my tears are falling to the floor in slow motion, just like before. I look at my Dad in despair, wondering whether I'm awake or dreaming. Wondering if I'm crazy!

"Seth, listen to me. You're dreaming right now and you must wake up! It's time to come home."

Then a voice: "Seth, Jamie, you both must pay attention now." "Dad did you here that?" My father turns his head in the direction of the voice.

"Yes, Seth, I heard it, and it sounded just like my guide." "Do we have the same guide?"

The voice again: "Listen to me both of you. I don't have time to explain. Go to the window and look outside."

My father and I go quickly to the widow and peer outside. "Dad, it's the black storm of nothing. It's mixing with our reality and will surely separate us. We must do something!" I say, knowing now that I must be dreaming if the black storm of sickness is coming.

"Seth," my guide says urgently, "Do you remember what I told you the last time you encountered the storm?"

"That's it! We must feel love right now before it gets to us." I embrace my father, remembering the Golden City and all its wonder and beauty, imagining everything about it and the love I felt when I was there.

"Seth, what do I do? I'm so afraid I might lose you again. I don't want to wake up. I still have so many things to tell you about reality."

I hold my father even closer, knowing that I have the power to take us to the Golden City. Pulling him down with me to the floor, I get into a cross-legged position and place my hands on his head. "Dad, think of nothing but love."

I visualize the Golden City and all the light beings and winged beings that were dancing with the crouching beings. A golden light begins to appear in my hands.

My father looks at me and smiles. "Is that the same light you used the last time we met?"

"Yes!" Now I know we're on our way to the Golden City. The blackness of the storm slowly encompasses the house, fading everything to night, and leaving only the glow that illuminates between my father and me.

"Seth, is it over?" he asks.

I looked around. Pitch-black darkness surrounds us, but I can see my father's face glowing in the light of the soft glow that lies between us.

"Is it over?" he asks again.

"Dad, we're ok. We didn't split apart as I thought we would. We're ok."

"Good job both of you! I'm very impressed that you stayed together and were able to generate enough love so fast. I truly thought that you were going to split up."

Light begins to filter in all around us, like the sun coming up on a moonless night. I see the Golden City, shimmering with beauty, just as I remember it. My father stares at it in awe.

"Dad, it's wonderful!"

"I can't believe I'm at the Golden City! How did you do it, Seth?" "Jamie, Seth has the power to travel through all dimensions. That's how he was able to contact you and heal you with the golden light."

"What? Dad, are you sick?"

"No son, not anymore." My father says, and then looks at me very seriously. "You don't know, do you?" "Know what"?

"Seth, don't you remember the accident"?

"I only remember what happened in our last lucid dream. It was just a dream, wasn't it? I was giving you some golden light, and then I woke up here in this room where I was meditating with the crystal balls."

"That's what I was trying to tell you back there. The accident was real. It happened three years ago back on earth. I was paralyzed for three years until last night when you gave me the golden light."

My father looks directly into my eyes and says, “And Seth, listen to me, you’ve been in a coma for the past three years.”

I look at my father and feel both joy and relief. “Then you really didn’t die! This is all a dream! The whole thing has been a dream!”

Our guide interrupts: “Seth, remember what I told you about the changes that are going to happen? Remember the cosmic being and Amber?”

I see my father growing very worried.

“I do, but if this is really a dream and I’m in a coma, then all I have to do is wake up and I’ll really be back on earth.” “That’s right, Seth. That’s what I’ve been trying to tell you.” My father says in a serious voice, almost as if he’s angry.

“Dad, don’t be negative. You must not use your negative emotion or . . .”

My father begins to fade away. “Seth.”

“Dad!”

“Seth wake up! Come back to me!” he says as he disappears. Devastated, I look at the Golden City. A beam of light is coming toward me.

“Seth, you’re very important to the transformation of the cosmic being,” my guide says.

“But what about my father and my life back on earth?” “Have you ever been in love?”

“No.”

“Love is the most powerful energy. It governs all planes of existence. There are only a few beings in all of creation that can do what you can do with love. When love is combined with the power of unity, then true love, in the form of an angel, is created. Don’t you want to become an angel?”

I think about the inside of the Golden City and remember how totally comfortable I was in the presence of the light beings and winged beings. I wonder they were angels. Could I really become one of those beautiful beings?

Suddenly I see a form is coming toward me. My eyes widen with joy. There she is!

“Amber!” Her name is all I can manage to say, as her radiant beauty overwhelms me. I stare into her greenish blue eyes, and feel their illuminating light pierce my body. Long, shining, jet-black hair flows down from her head to cover the silken skin of her naked form. Her body glows with a faint purple aura.

I’m mesmerized as Amber greets me by placing her hand on my shoulder, instantly my desperate state of confusing is gone. “Seth,

I’ve been waiting for this moment for a very long time.”

Chapter 5
The uniting

Chapter 5

The Uniting

I stare into Amber's eyes, and instantly feel a deep connection, as if I've known her for a very long time.

"Seth, do you feel it?" she asks. Her voice is warm and soothing. My stomach starts to tingle as her words echo through my head. Laughter and love swirl inside my stomach and radiate out like a storm, gathering strength and power with every second.

"Yes, Amber, I can feel it. What's happening?"

She doesn't speak, and the silence extends like an eternity of lifetimes. I know the feeling I have in my stomach is directly connected to the Golden City.

Still staring into each other's eyes, Amber places her other hand on my other shoulder, then slides both hands down my back, pulling me to her and off the ground. We embrace me with our bodies and our spirits. Engulfed in intense emotion, we float in the air as one being, connected in every way. A bright yellow light bursts out of our stomachs and surrounds us in an aura of protective energy. Nothing in the entire universe could penetrate this force field, and I know that as long as I'm with Amber I'll be safe and never alone.

Then my whole body is frozen, paralyzed from head to toe and the same feeling of love and welfare that I had while in the Golden City grips me stronger than before, leaving me helpless once again. "Seth, this is the power of spiritual light. Don't analyze it or try to figure it out. Don't judge it. Where we're going there is no ego, only true self."

I hear Amber's words, but I can't consciously understand what she's telling me. Then a deep part of me begins to feel her words, and I understand on a level I never knew existed. I forget everything that I've based my life on, and let go of all things. I let go of who I think I am.

Our bodies begin to move in a strange but beautiful way. Bonded together from head to toe, we fly though the air like two dolphins swimming in the ocean during their mating dance. We sway back and forth, thrusting through the air, We're creating pure love as we dance the dance of creation. Without the need for physical penetration, every movement sends a powerful orgasm surging through us like a bolt of lightning. Faster and faster we fly though the air in perfect harmony.

The love I experienced in the Golden City is now in my mind and flowing through my soul. I think if I had this feeling while in the Golden City, I wouldn't have had to leave so abruptly.

Amber smiles as if she can read my thoughts. I realize that Amber is a part of me now, and I'm a part of her. I think, "Amber, can you read my thoughts?" A voice, like the voice I hear when my guide speaks to me, comes from nowhere and everywhere. "Yes, Seth. I can hear everything you think, and feel everything you feel."

Realizing how closely connected Amber and I really are, I feel almost embarrassed that I'm with another being who knows my thoughts and feels what I feel. I know now how important it is to express only love, because if I express anything else, Amber and I would split apart. "You're right, Seth," Amber 'says' with her thoughts.

I feel I'll never be alone again as long as I can feel love. "Seth, only a few people in the entire universe have the ability to go where you have been, and only two people in the entire universe are going to the place we're going now. What might happen and where we're going is not important. It's only important that you be in the present moment at all times."

"Amber, if that's will keep us together, I won't think or feel anything other than what's happening right now in this moment." How strange it is for another person to know exactly what I'm feeling and thinking while it's happening!

"What did I tell you about that?" Amber replies telepathically, sending a wave of emotion that hits my stomach and makes me realize that she's very serious about me staying in the moment. I focus on the moment, letting go of all that I believe and have believed in my entire life.

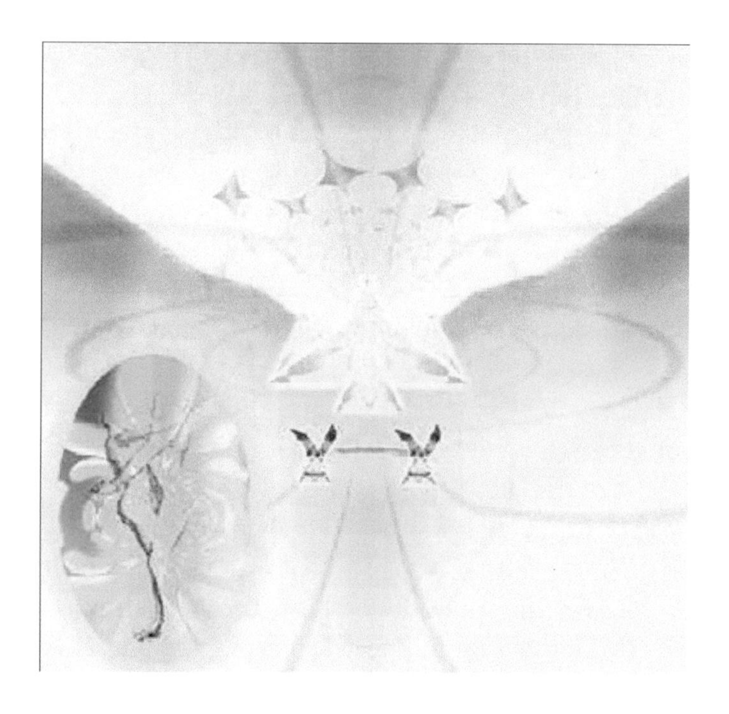

"Look Seth. There it is."

I look in the direction Amber is pointing and see the Golden City. It's more beautiful than ever.

"We'll enter the City in a completely different way than how you entered before, a way you or I could never enter alone. You're about to go to a place you could never have possibly imagined. It's very important that you remember what I told you about staying in the moment."

Suddenly I realize the importance of feeling nothing but love, letting go of all things, and letting good guide me into whatever lies next.

"Amber, where is my guide?" I ask, wondering why he hasn't spoken to me in some time now.

"Seth, your guide is an angel, and he has his own path to follow. If you need guidance as we enter the Golden City, communicate to me. I am your guide now your angel and you are mine, as you will soon see."

I'm so filled with a feeling of total security and comfort that my mind doesn't question anything Amber has just told me.

"Very good, Seth! That's wonderful! You're doing great!" I hear Amber with my mind. This will take some getting used to!

"Don't worry about it. You'll do fine," Amber 'says'. "As you learn to calm your mind, you'll find that this form of communication is very effective."

I take comfort in her thought, realizing that I trust her totally. "Seth, it's time for you to purify your soul. This is unlike any purification process you have ever done before. We're going to use spiritual alchemy to purify every part of you. Then, once you've been purified, the transforming process will begin. That's when we can enter the Golden City and go to where the master angels are."

"What am I going to transform into?"

"Always remember that you are always you, no matter what happens. Spiritual alchemy can transform your entire being to express as a pure spiritual essence, but it can't alter who you are. Spiritual transformation allows you to move much more deeply into yourself - your true self. Once you've purified all parts of you, we'll go together to a vibrational level that will allow us to enter a very special place within the Golden City."

"What is this special place? I thought I'd seen it all when I entered the city the last time."

"Seth, you have lots to do and lots to learn!" Amber's laugh is like beautiful music.

We start to slow down the waving motion that has been propelling us through the air in such harmony, and I have time to think that communicating entirely through telepathy seems so real, as if we were really speaking to each other. I feel a bit confused about it.

"As long as you don't think about it, it'll soon come naturally you won't get confused," Amber says' in a soft voice.

We're now completely stopped, suspended motionless near the Golden City, and still in our embrace.

"It's time to begin the purification of your soul."

Long, stained glass panes of beautiful artwork form around us, creating a kind of glass church whose walls are filled with images of thousands of angels. This luminous, round structure seems to be telling a story. Then I realize that I'm witnessing the energy within the Golden City and how the angels work together to do their great work.

"Seth, you are very brilliant to have put that together with one glance," Amber communicates to me excitedly.

"I only noticed it because the last time I was here I saw the same thing." I point my finger to a section of the round glass wall that has an exact replica of the half dolphin/half human beings I had seen earlier. And directly below them are the crouching beings! The walls are painted exactly as they were when I was last in the Golden City, only this time I know that the winged beings, the crouching beings, and the light beings are all angels.

I look closer and am amazed to see that the walls aren't made of glass at all, and they're not solid. When I look at the entire wall with my peripheral vision, I can see that the glass church is moving like an animation movie. It's a replica of the Golden City, moving in harmony.

"Seth, there's more to it than you thought," Amber communicates, as if she's getting ready to fill me in on what the Golden City is really about.

"Yes, it's time for you to know the work of the Golden City and how you fit into all of this. Now have a seat." Instantly, two chairs appear right next to us.

"Wait, Amber. Before you go any further, I want to know how you create things like that."

"My love, the world we're in right now is based on a predestined harmony that is one with spirituality. It may appear to you that I'm creating what's happening in front of us, but in actuality, everything that you and I experience is already going to happen, and has been happening for a long, long time. The only difference is that in this world we're joining in and becoming part of destiny, as you're about to see."

I sit down on the chair with eyes wide, staring at Amber like a child waiting for a gift.

"Before we start your purification, I need all your attention because what you're about to learn may come as a surprise. So get ready."

I relax and give Amber my complete, undivided attention. I know this is going to answer a lot of questions I've had for a long time.

"Seth, look at the wall, about half way down from the top, and tell me what you see."

The entire wall is moving and changing, but my eyes almost unconsciously focus one particular spot. To my amazement I see my hometown and my house! Even though I still feel that I'm an important part of this plan, I wonder why I'm seeing my house on earth on this wall!

"Relax and watch the wall, Seth. The transformation is going to start right now."

At that moment, the wall begins to move and animate like a giant screen in an amazing movie theatre, and I'm somehow the star of the show. I watch my hometown with great curiosity as Amber starts to narrate this wonderful movie.

Suddenly, I'm in the state of mind that happens just before falling asleep. Knowing that this is a critical moment, I relax and let Amber guide my experience, letting go of all earthly concepts. "That's great, Seth. Stay relaxed and comfortable within yourself. Let go of all you know about life and religion. A totally new awareness is being born within you. Now, wake up," Amber says telepathically.

I feel a pulling sensation throughout my body. I'm still staring at my home back at earth, my mind's eye surrounded by this 'movie', but the rest of me is here with Amber, next to the Golden City. I'm experiencing two places at one time.

"Now is the time, Seth. Watch closely and learn," Amber communicates to me very intensely.

I enter the house I was born in, and see myself as a baby boy playing. There are winged beings - angels filled with light hovering above me. They seem to be very interested in my wellbeing.

"Seth, that's you as a baby boy, and those are your angels." "What do you mean my angels?"

"Unless you're able to travel between worlds using out-of-body experiences or lucid dreaming, one plane of existence is all that is experienced. But, as you now know, the earth isn't the only place in the universe. This place is the unseen world, and the angels who are taking so much interest in you are from this unseen place you call the dream world."

With a keen perception, I look deeper into the earth's energy and realize that the earth is surrounded with hundreds of thousands of angels, all talking with different people and shooting sparkling light from their hands. I watch the light beam up into the heavens to one place of unity - the Golden City.

The angels who are watching over me are also communicating to me and then sending a message up into the heavens. They're communicating with many other people as well.

"The angels are working as guides, helping people with their decisions. Do you remember when you were around 13 years old and you kept hearing and feeling sensations that you thought was your intuition?"

"Yes, I remember that well because it was a turning point in my life. It was the first time I felt confident in myself because I knew my intuition would never let me down. All I had to do was listen to it and everything would be ok."

Suddenly I'm watching a moment in my life when I was almost hit by a car while crossing the street. My inner voice kept me safe. I listened to my inner self, and then the angles were there, at least five of them, whispering in my ear. Every time I had a thought, they would communicate with beams of light up into the heavens. All those times I thought my inner voice was really me, and I was guiding myself through my tough times, it was really the angels who were guiding me.

"That's right, Seth. You have never been alone. No spiritual being is alone as long as it can listen to the suggestions of love. The angels only communicate love and good to all. They keep track of who's listening, then send the information to the Golden City where it gets processed, allowing the cosmic being to progress and evolve."

I'm watching now with my entire vision, my eyes taking in every image. I realize that all life on earth, as well as in any other place, is important.

"You're starting to understand that everything is connected, Seth. Soon you'll see how important your connection is to the changes that are happening throughout the universe."

All the images I see begin to move in harmony with a beautiful, soothing music. I see the universe working like a choreographed musical, with every part important to every other part and to the greater picture. Everything is growing and expanding to one rhythm that I feel course through my body. Information begins to pour into me, and I realize that I'm experiencing the inner workings of the cosmic being, which functions in the same manner as the human body, progressing through growth, change and evolution. "Everything is part of the cosmic being, which evolves with wisdom and knowledge. A human being evolves from a new born, to an adolescent, to an adult, then to old age, and finally passes on in death to start the next stage of his or her development. Like a human, the cosmic being has reached old age and is about to transform and move into its new stage of development. The unity of your soul and my soul is the last transformative event that will give the cosmic being the remaining bit of knowledge and wisdom it needs to transform and move on."

My eyes grow wide in amazement as I realize how important my part is to the life of this universe. I remember my father telling me: "Angels, Seth. It's all about angels."

"Your father was right, Seth. You are one of the very few souls that have accepted true love, and that love has brought you here to me so we can fulfill our destiny together and become an angel." "You and I are going to become an angel?" I stare at Amber, delighted at the prospect of becoming and angel, but very unsure as to how that will happen.

"Relax. Concentrate on your feelings of unconditional love, and it'll be OK."

The music intensifies and the images around me get very vivid. I fill my body with the same sensation I had back in the Golden City when everything I was seeing and experiencing was connected to my emotions. As the feeling of unconditional love gets stronger, my experience comes together.

"That's it, Seth! You're doing wonderfully! "I faintly hear from Amber. My complete concentration is on feeling nothing but love.

Then angels are flying around in every direction, moving in unison to the music and intertwined with my emotions. As my love grows, I understand how the angels live in the unseen world we humans call the subconscious. They communicate to humans through thought, transmitting an inner intuitive inner sense that changes the outcome of almost any destination. Millions of angels receive messages from the Golden City and send them directly into the thoughts of human beings on earth.

My attention shifts to the Golden City, where I see six magnificent angels sitting in a meditative position around a large beam of light. They're much larger than any other angel I've seen.

"Those are archangels, Seth, and we'll be going to them together as one very soon."

I suddenly realize what's about to happen to me, and at the same time I see the whole plan. The archangels are sending a message telepathically into the large beam of light. That message is filtered out to the crouching beings in the form of colored light. The crouching beings send the message's colored light to the half dolphin/half human beings, who pass it to the millions of light beings. The light beings will carry the message into the thoughts of human beings on earth, allowing love to be spread like pollen, unseen, but ensuring the survival all life on all planes of existence.

I get an image of a flower blooming with all its exact, geometrical parts, and know that something as perfect as a flower blooming has to be created by something. I realize how important I really am to the whole picture of life in this universe, and focus all my attention on the archangels who are playing one of the dominant roles in the creation of life on earth.

"And earth is exactly where we're going, Seth. Soon we'll become an archangel, creating eternal love for the rest of the human race to experience.

"Now listen closely. As you see, there are six archangels in that circle. One is missing. The seventh angel will be the combination of you and I, united as one. As one being combined with the power of love, we'll create a seventh master angel who will not only contribute to the awakening spirituality on earth, but will give the cosmic being the final bit of information to transform on its path of evolution.

"You must remember how important you are to all life so that you can make the final step in becoming one with love." Amber speaks softly but firmly, as if I'm about to go to a place very far away.

"Amber, Where am I going? What do I do with my love to make this happen?"

Suddenly I'm lying on a table. Amber is standing over me, her beauty as overwhelming as ever. She looks into my eyes, and I feel her hands on my stomach.

"Seth, as I pass my loving energy through you, a healing process will begin within you and you'll begin to heal yourself. Then we'll begin to unite, becoming an angel." She says this will complete love and confidence.

"You must remember not to forget me."

A golden light passes through Amber's hands and into my body. Somehow, instead of feeling love, I'm scared, then filled with fear. Amber begins to fade. Everything begins to fade to blackness. I can barely hear her words, "You must remember . . ."

Blinding light strikes my eyes, and a blurry figure waves in front of me. Slowly my vision, hearing, and the rest of my physical senses come back. A nurse is jumping up and down in front of me.

"He is awake! He is awake!"

I look around the room. I'm in a hospital. My father is standing next to me, and takes me in a loving embraces. Tears run down my face, partly because I'm overjoyed to see him, and in partly because I'm terribly confused. I turn my head and see a beautifully radiant woman standing next to my father.

"Amber! Are you really here?" I slightly push my father aside. "No, honey. Don't be silly. I'm your mother. I'm here with you at last!"

I'm both utterly disappointed and extremely amazed that I hear my mother's voice.

"Mom?" I say as tears flow down my face. My mother hugs me. The solidness of her body against mine tells me that I'm awake and she's not dead.

"You're alive!" I shout, shaking uncontrollably with emotion.

I look at my father and say again "You're alive!"

"Seth, what are you talking about?" My mother looks at me with great concern on her face. "You were in a car accident and have been unconscious for the past two hours. We rushed down here the minute we heard. The doctor said you had a minor concussion and should wake soon, so we've been hear waiting for you to wake up."

I look around. Everything seems so real. A heavy feeling comes over me, like I'm being crushed by a ton of water. I pick up a piece of paper and scream out the words that I see on it: "IS THIS A DREAM?"

My parents look at me like I'm crazy. A doctor comes rushing in. "Hello, Seth. I see that you're awake. Did you have some dreams while you were unconscious? Don't worry, everything will be fine. It's perfectly normal to be a bit confused. You are not hurt as badly as you could have been in that accident, but a bit of rehabilitation should do wonders for you."

"What about Amber and the Golden City?" I ask, terrified.

Now the doctor as well as my parents look at me like I'm crazy. Then the doctor turns to my parents and says, "Don't worry about this. He must have had some very interesting dreams while he was unconscious. He should be fine in a couple of days."

When he turns to look at me, I get a feeling that I shouldn't trust him.

"Seth, do you know where you are?" he asks in a serious tone.

I look at my hands, then look up at the doctor. "I'm in a hospital."

"Good, Seth. Now tell me how old you are."

Suddenly I'm very confused. I don't know how old I am.

"I can't remember. As a matter of a fact, I have no idea what year it is!"

"Seth, that's just fine. You don't need to worry right now. Just tell me the last thing you can remember. It's OK. Take your time." The doctor sits down in the chair next to the bed, acting quite pleasant, but I know that he's as confused as I am.

I try to think of the last thing I remember, and instantly I begin to get flashes of a little girl in my mind. Uncontrollably, I yell out "Samantha!" and in a flash I start to remember many things about my life. My mind downloads millions of memories about life as it is now here on earth, and with every new memory about where I am right now, everything about Amber, the Golden City, and angels begins to fade. I cry in confusion and relief as the most real memory finishes rumbling within my mind.

I stare at the doctor and ask, "Where is Samantha? Can I see her?"

"That is exactly what I thought. Seth, all you needed was a few moments to fully wake up. It's OK. It's completely normal to have a bit of amnesia after the blow you took to your head." The doctor tells me in a soft voice.

My father and mother move aside as the doctor scoots his char back a bit, unblocking my view of a little girl standing behind all of them. Samantha runs to me with arms wide, wanting a hug from her father. Everything moves in slow motion, but when she hugs me, love overwhelms me and I forget everything about the dreams I had about Amber and the Golden City. I know that this must be real because I can remember everything the moment Samantha gave me her unconditional love.

I look at the doctor and my parents. “Everything will be OK. I’m fine. I remember now.”

Slowly, memories of raising my little girl begin to form in my mind. Then a dajavue comes over me and I know I’ve experienced all of this before.

My little girl begins to transform, growing older with every second. I stare at her as she becomes a grown woman holding my hands. I look at my hands and they’re the hands of an old man. In that instant I know what’s happening to me.

In my wonderful daughter’s eyes I see a slight reflection of Amber standing over me, passing energy through my body. I start to remember everything that happened to me in my entire life, and realize that I’m dying as an old man. I can’t move my body, but my mind is as sharp as a fresh razor.

I look at my hands again, staring into every wrinkle filled with memories of my long life. I feel a deep comfort knowing that I’m 96 years old and that I’ve had a wonderful life. It’s time for me to pass on to the other side.

I’m incredibly excited, realizing that all I’ve experienced up to this moment was all about letting go of the things that I’m attached to so that I could go in peace. I look at Samantha and know that I’ve let go of everything else and now I have to let her go too. She looks back at me, as if she knows what’s going to happen, and says, “Seth, you’re doing great! Don’t fight what’s happening. Let it all go. It’s time.”

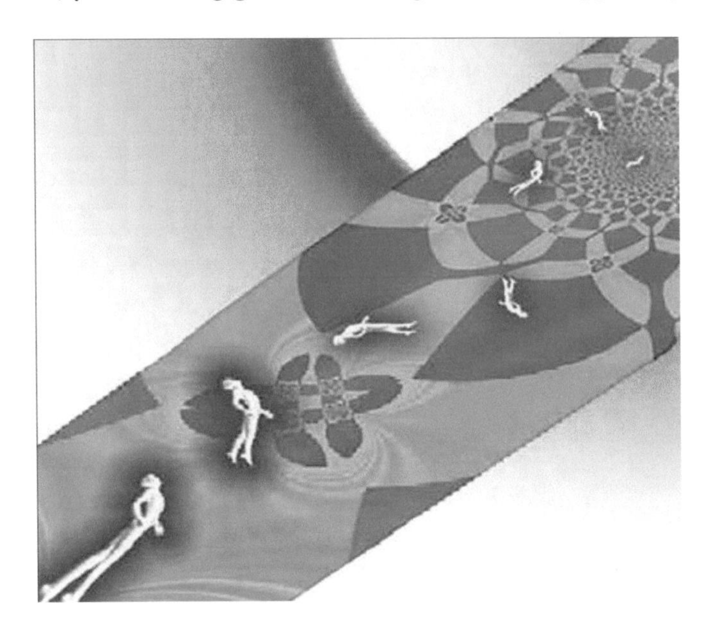

I see a wonderful light glowing behind her, filling the whole room. Everything begins to fade into a large tunnel. I feel a pulling sensation in my stomach as I start to float away. My life flashes in front of my eyes, and I completely understand that all the experiences with the isolation floatation tank, lucid dreaming, my father dying, and the coma was all preparation for what's lying ahead. I know that the only thing at this point that's real in my life is Amber, the Golden City, the angels, and the cosmic being.

On the other side of the tunnel I see myself as a young boy with Amber extending her hand to me. I know that my journey in the afterlife is ready to begin and I won't be coming back to the place I considered the real world. I'm excited that I was able to let go of my attachments, allowing me to have a completely aware death. I know my adventures are going to be wonderful because I can now unite with my great work by fully becoming one with my new life with Amber within the Golden City.

Chapter 6
THE
TRANSFORMATION

Chapter 6

The Transformation

I'm fully out of my body, floating up into the luminous tunnel and spinning slowly in a clockwise direction and I drift further and further from the earth and closer to Amber and my true self. I know I'll never be a human again.

The lighted tunnel seems to go on forever, growing larger the closer I get to Amber. I feel like I'm hundreds of miles away from both my old self and my new self.

I'm floating up and up, wondering what's going to happen next, when flashback images remind me of the floatation tank, the lucid dreaming, my father's diary, the car crash, my angel guiding me through parts of the Golden City, Amber, and the cosmic being. All of it was preparation for this moment. Even though I seem to be so far away from Amber and the earth, I'm comforted that everything up to this point was a process of letting go, and letting go allowed my dying body to forgive and forget. My long life's experiences on earth happened in only a moment of universal time.

I'm so far from my old life now that I no longer see anything except the tunnel that stretches on and on forever, fading into a wonderful golden light. I look toward my new life, excited and ready to take on all the responsibilities of my new existence with Amber and the angels.

Far off in the distance, I see two figures. As I draw closer to the figures, I see myself as a young man. Amber is passing different colored light through different parts of my body. She slowly turns her head in my direction and stares into my eyes, gently waving at me to come to her.

Still floating and slowly spinning in a clockwise motion, I get nearer to my new self. Amber, looking even more beautiful than I remembered, mesmerizes me as I float right through her and into my new young body.

I open my eyes and I'm lying on a table looking up at Amber. Excited and full of love and joy, I sit up, feeling a bit dizzy, and remember that Amber and I can hear each other's thoughts.

She looks at me and smiles. "Seth, you did great! You had a much easier time than I did. It took me much longer to let go of my old life."

I smile back at her, comforted by her words. "Thank you for helping me through the transition. I couldn't have done it without knowing that you were waiting for me. It's strange, but I don't miss my old life at all. It's like a distant memory that's quickly fading." I get up and stand beside her. She's very close to me, and I feel that it's time. "What do you want me to do?" I ask, looking deeply into her eyes.

"For the next few moments don't think of anything but love.

Keep your thoughts focused on love and nothing else."

She wraps her arms, then her legs, tightly around me. Naked, we float up into the air.

Using all my focus to think and feel nothing but love, a combination of sexual sensation and pure love completely engulfs us. "Put your hands on mine," Amber says, lifting her arms up over her head. She's very calm and relaxed. I lift up my arms and interlace my fingers with hers. We're stretched out fully, touching feet and hands.

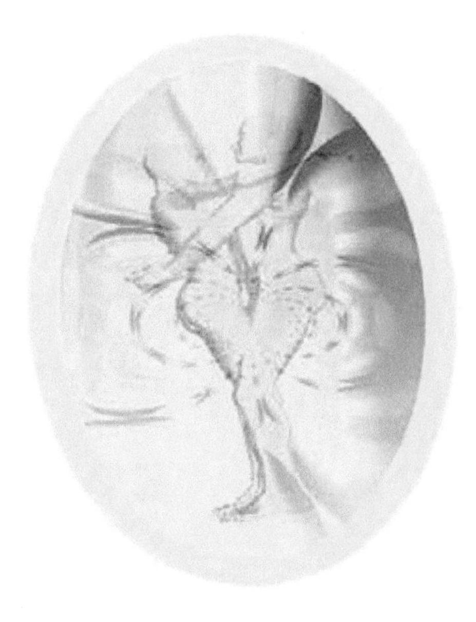

Still staring into her beautiful eyes, I slowly penetrate her. I'm all sensation. Golden light is flowing through and around us, joining us together, merging our bodies physically, mentally, emotionally, and spiritually. We're floating in a cocoon of golden light, and I realize that she's no longer pressed to me. She's disappeared. Amber and I have become one.

"I'm right here, Seth" Amber says, surprising me because I can't see her. Then I realize where she is.

"That's right, Seth. We did it! We're one now. I'm you and you're me. We're one being!"

"Amber, you can still hear my thoughts!" My hands have changed into white light.

"Yes. That's why we got familiar with communicating as one before," she answers. "Now it seems quite natural, doesn't it?" "This is amazing!" I exclaim. "You're talking to me, but you're part of my thoughts, and I must be part of yours."

The golden light cocoon fades, leaving 'us', the being that Amber and I have become, standing in front of the Golden City.

"Look at that!" I point to a reflection on a wall. We've transformed into a beautiful, pure white, winged being. With eyes wide and heart pounding, we stare in amazement at the reflection of the being we've become.

I'm amazed that I feel Amber all around me and inside me, filling me comfort, energy and joy I never felt as a human. I realize at that moment that being alone is an illusion that humans create.

"You can feel what I'm feeling, can't you?"

"Oh, yes, Seth. We've just made love floating in space, with our arms and legs wrapped all around each other, and now I can feel every part of you and it's wonderful. I've never felt this comfortable in my entire life."

"I feel the same way," I say, as excitement surges through our newly created form. I feel that Amber and I as one can do anything in the entire universe.

"Seth, we must find our path so that we can continue our work and keep focused on the Golden City and the wishes of the cosmic being."

"Hey you guys - over here!" A voice comes from the Golden City. We recognize the voice, but we can't see anything.

"Over here!" repeats the voice. Amber and I look up to see another being of pure light high above us, fading in and out, zipping around and twirling down toward us.

"Don't look so surprised, you guys. It's me, your guide Joseph! How could you forget me?"

Amber and I suddenly realize that Joseph has been guiding both of us all our lives. We're amazed that we finally know his name!

"Amber, can you believe it? It's my guide and his name is Joseph!" I exclaim.

"He's my guide too! Without him I would never have found you. He helped me through the hardest times in my life." Amber is very excited.

"Now calm down both of you. I'll explain." Joseph lands right next to us, staring into our big eyes, just as excited to see us as we are to see him and to hear his voice.

"Let me look at you," he says, eyeing us with fascination. "It's incredible. You've transformed into a much more beautiful angel than I ever expected. The love you have for each other is very strong indeed!"

"We've been in a state of ecstasy ever since the transformation happened."

"Yes, I can see that," Joseph says, smiling. "Seth, you were able to let go of your human family to join us here in the afterworld."

"Once I realized I was a dying old man and all the experiences I had in my life were a part of the letting go process, it was simple," I say to my guide.

"That's very good, because most people get to the point of death and won't let go of their family and their things." Joseph is very impressed.

"What happens to them?" I ask.

"When a human passes to the afterworld at the moment of death, they have an opportunity to let go of everything so that they can begin a new life. Each person is different, and the amount of healing that takes place during this time of transition determines where they go and what they become next. If they can raise their vibration during this time of transition, they'll meet with their counter part, like you and Amber met. But if they hold on to anything in their life's experience while transforming, they can get stuck in that reality for as long as it takes them to remember what's really happening. Seth, did you think that all the experiences you went through to get here took a long time?"

"Yes I do," I reply. "It was a very long time, and it all seemed so real."

"You had some special attention and help from me and some of the other angelic beings," Joseph explains. "And it certainly was worth all the extra effort. But many others don't get this special attention."

"Joseph, what special attention did I get that others don't get? Why can't everyone transform into an angel like Amber and I did?"

"The cosmic being is very old now, and getting ready to pass on and transform into its next stage of evolution, just as you've passed on and became an angel. As a matter of fact, the cosmic being is at the exact point in its evolution that you just experienced. You see, Gabriel, all beings on earth are part of a very important plan in this process of evolution. As the cosmic being passes on into its next world, it will have to make choices and let go of the past. That will create a healing process which will allow the cosmic being to transform into a more spiritual being, just as you have transformed into an angel."

"Amber, did you hear what Joseph just called us?" I ask, excited to have a name that connects us together.

"Yes I did, Seth. Does that mean that our name is 'Gabriel'?" Amber asks. Hearing our thoughts, Joseph replies, "Amber, you and Seth are one now. If you're going to develop your power together, then you need to have a name. That name is 'Gabriel'."

A new bond has been created between Amber and me as we realize that we are one being, with one name.

"Listen, Gabriel. This is important," Joseph continues. "The cosmic being has passed into the dream world. Seth, do you remember when you were having those lucid dreams and trying to figure out which reality was the real one? That's exactly what the cosmic being is doing right now. It's letting go."

"Is that why the earth is so out of control?" I ask anxiously. "Is that why I had those experiences where everything was being destroyed by that powerful storm?"

"Seth, when you and Amber were living on earth, you both were very old and in the hospital. You don't know what's been happening on earth during the past couple of months," Joseph says gently.

"What's happening back on earth? Is everyone and everything ok?" Amber and I ask.

"It's not ok on earth, Gabriel," Joseph replies, very serious now. "The imbalance in the world has created a problem for the cosmic being. In fact, this particular being has been sick for quite a while now."

"Do you mean that there's more than one cosmic being?" Gabriel asks.

"Oh, yes! The earth is one being, but there are millions of solar systems with planets that have life on them, and each has a cosmic being counterpart. Each cosmic being lives in a cosmic world, growing from children into adults, then dying to become more evolved, just as any human being. But this particular being became very sick when the humans cells of its body stopped working in unity, depleting the earth of its life out of greed and the need for dominant power. Human beings have lost their ability to work in unity with the earth, and the suffering of the earth as well as the suffering of human beings has made this particular cosmic being very ill, which has drawn a lot of attention from the other cosmic beings. The earth and its cosmic counterpart are being healed in a place on the cosmic plane of existence much like the hospital you were in on earth. Your role in this healing is what you've been preparing for, Gabriel."

As Amber and I realize what Joseph is saying, Gabriel is overwhelmed. Joseph puts his hand on Gabriel's shoulder. "Everything will be ok, Gabriel. "The angelic beings gave you so much attention and support because you're the one who's going to complete the healing process that the cosmic beings have started. Human beings are having a problem moving through the stage of evolution where death happens. They're not letting go of their life experiences at the point of death, so they get trapped in a long cycle of healing, postponing the creation of angelic beings. As a result, there are fewer guides to help humans in their evolutionary progression.

"But both of you were different," Joseph adds quickly. "You had a very high capacity to feel and use your pure love. We also knew that both of you, as counterparts for each other, could unite into one being, so we gave you extra attention. That pure love transformed into you, Gabriel, the master angel who can heal a cosmic being." Joseph stands back, looking at Gabriel almost in reverence.

Still very confused, Amber and I look at Joseph, and as Gabriel, ask, "What do the cosmic beings want me to do? I'm here to use my power as an angel for whatever is asked of me."

Joseph swoops up into the air and swirls around Gabriel. "Well, Gabriel, people have become so alone and individualistic that they've started to ignore some of our best angels. Do you remember the crouching beings back in the Golden City? The glowing white angels get information from human beings and give it to the crouching beings, allowing them to do their dance of creation. The intellectual beings can pick up the energy emitted from that dance of creation and put it together in the proper language for the master angels to understand."

Amber and I don't remember any intellectual beings. Gabriel shakes his head and says, "What intellectual beings are you talking about, Joseph?"

"The half human/half dolphin beings that you, Seth, encountered while you were in the Golden City," Joseph replies. As Amber and I remember the experience I had with the dolphin beings, Gabriel understands and opens his eyes wide with excitement.

"Gabriel, do you see how the interaction between Amber and Seth creates your consciousness so you can carry out your great work and evolve? The information that all humans give to all angels makes the cosmic being grow. That's why this particular cosmic being is sick - it's missing a big part of itself because humans aren't having that communication on earth. Seth and Amber, when you were human, your bodies could only be healthy if every part was communicating and working together with every other part. Can you imagine what would happen if you couldn't relate to your stomach and it never told you when you were hungry? You'd get very sick! The Amber parts and the Seth parts of you, Gabriel, worked together and united in harmony, allowing you to understand the true language of spiritual love. You, my great friend, are uniquely capable of getting the lost information so that the cosmic being can communicate it to its healers, allowing them to heal the problem that the cosmic being is going through."

"How do I do that?" Gabriel asks, almost overwhelmed by Amber and my amazement at finally hearing our mission.

Joseph gives him a huge hug, sending energy through every part of Amber and me. "Don't worry, Gabriel. We have friends everywhere, even on earth, who understand the spiritual language of love. The problem is that, at this time on earth, no one is able to communicate what they need to the cosmic being because of the lack of angels. So you have to go back to earth, get the information, and communicate it to the cosmic being yourself. There are places on earth that still hold the information that the cosmic healers need to complete their work and for the cosmic being to heal itself. These places are the ancient ruins left from the Maya and Egyptian people."

Amber and I think back to our visits to Mexico and Egypt, when we explored all the pyramids. We don't remember a cosmic language of love.

"I'm confused, Joseph. Tell me more," Gabriel says.

"With man's limited perception, the full meaning of the pyramids cannot be understood. Ancient people understood the natural simplicity of things. Today, technology and greed have made it almost impossible for human beings to fully grasp the overall picture of life. That's why you must go back to the places were the ancient people of earth left the cosmic message of love, and communicate that message directly back to the cosmic being. Then the cosmic being can heal, transform, and progress as planned. This will create harmony in the human world on earth and everywhere else. Great times are coming for all things, and you're a very important part of this plan."

"I'll do it, Joseph. I'll do whatever I can," Gabriel says, realizing how important this is, although Amber and I feel very small in this great plan.

"Great!" Joseph exclaims. "You must go to the great pyramid in Egypt and to the Yucatan peninsula were the Mayan ruins of Pelenque and Tulum are, and then to Stonehenge."

Gabriel bows toward Joseph. Amber and I are excited to see what these places will look like through Gabriel's eyes.

"What do I do when I get to these places?" asks Gabriel. "Your ability to understand the cosmic language of love through the interaction of Amber and Seth will give you the answer to your question. Now get going!" Joseph replies with some urgency.

Gabriel reaches out and hugs Joseph tightly, feeling that this may be the last time he'll see his guide. Amber and I are sad at this thought, but excited at the thought of going on this amazing journey.

"Good-bye, Joseph, and thank you for everything. I'll do as you say and everything will be ok."

Joseph hugs him in return. "Good-bye, Gabriel. Have a great journey."

Amber and I start to bring up images of the great pyramid of Egypt in Gabriel's mind, allowing him to visualize what it looks like. Gabriel sees these images in his mind's eye, and with lightning speed and power, we're hovering above the great pyramid of Egypt, and Amber and I instantly understand what its purpose was for the ancient people of Egypt.

Gabriel's eyes are wide with excitement as he looks at huge beams of light coming directly from the tip of the three pyramid's and spreading out into a colored, circular shaped force field around the entire structure. In the many times Amber and I have been here, we never saw this force field, but we've been inside the pyramid and know the source of the golden light. This knowledge is instantly transferred to Gabriel's mind, and without delay he darts straight into the center of the pyramid where the king's chamber is.

Amber and I are familiar with the king's chamber, and know that when the sound 'OM' is chanted here, the echo of that sound creates different frequencies and vibrations that allow human beings to move into altered states of consciousness. When this information is sent to Gabriel, he begins to chant 'OM' very deep into his stomach.

The power of Gabriel's 'OM' shoots through us like a bolt of lightning. Then a doorway made of light appears right in front of him. On the other side of the doorway we see our second destination, Stonehenge, and understand that the ancient people were able to travel from one place to another by using the power of this incredible pyramid.

Gabriel suddenly sits down into a cross-legged position and closes his eyes. Amber and I don't understand what he's doing. We didn't give him any information that would create this behavior. He must be seeing something that we cannot.

Continuing to chant 'OM' louder and louder, Gabriel spreads his hands out wide as a bright light bolts from within his stomach and shoots out his hands, as if he's sending a signal to someone or something.

Amber and I suddenly realize that Gabriel is communicating to the cosmic being. At this same moment we also realize that Gabriel now has his own individuality, allowing him to understand and do things separately from the interaction that Amber and I have between us. More surprising is our realization that when Gabriel acts independently from us, his information is instantly sent to us.

Gabriel is using the energy field that surrounds the great pyramid as a magnet, tuning it to pick up all the love that human beings are feeling and sending that love to the cosmic being. A huge surge of universal love flies through us. Gabriel is doing the work of the thousands of angels who have been lost for so long. "Amber and Seth, can you understand me now?" We hear a voice coming from nowhere and everywhere.

"It is me, Gabriel. I can now communicate to myself, and you are my inner intuition."

"Gabriel, what do you hear from us?" I ask.

"Seth, I know that is you and I know that Amber is there too." "Yes, Gabriel, I am." Amber says.

A feeling of complete wholeness spreads through the three of us and we know that we all are separate but yet one.

"What did you just do, Gabriel?" I ask.

"I've just completed the first part of our task. All the pyramids were designed to pick up and hold the energy of spirituality and love within the golden force field that we encountered on the way in," Gabriel replies.

"Did the ancient people build these pyramids to absorb the spiritual energy from human beings so that it could be transferred to the cosmic being?"

"That's close, Amber. The spiritual, loving energy was not transferred to the cosmic being until I transferred it just now. It was used to create portals that humans could use to travel between worlds and travel to any part of the earth. The pyramids were used as a means of transportation, allowing the ancient people to go any place on earth as well as any place within the dream world. But I've found a new use for them. By directing my attention to the cosmic world, I can act as a medium to transfer the energy that's being picked up by the pyramids directly to the cosmic being. And the best part of it is that every time I filter this love through my body, I too begin to progress and evolve!"

Amber understands that by the time we're finished with this work, Gabriel will transform into the seventh master angel. "That's right," Gabriel says. "As I pass the universal love through my body, finishing the work that couldn't be completed because of the lack of angels, we'll all transform into the seventh master angel."

"Will the cosmic being heal as a result of receiving the information that's been lost for so long?"

"Yes, Seth. And as the cosmic being heals, human beings will begin to love each other once again, and more angels will be created.

This healing will create a change in cosmic consciousness that will result in more harmony and love, on earth as well as throughout the entire universe. . This cycle will put the cosmic plan back on its path," Gabriel explains.

"And all this will happen as we transform into the seventh master angel?"

"The changes for us will be very fast, Seth, but in terms of earth time, it won't be until the year 2012 that the cosmic way of life will

once again be back on the earth's physical plane."

Gabriel stands up, his meditation completed. "It's time to continue our journey," Amber and I hear his thought. He quickly walks through the doorway of light, and we're teleported to the ancient site of Stonehenge. A force field very similar to the one at the great pyramid is at the center of the giant stones.

"Amber, can you feel the energy?" I ask, curious as to what's happening to us.

"Yes, Seth. We're becoming one," Amber answers.

Gabriel says, "Every time I absorb the energy of these magical places, we're completing the evolution of the cosmic being, allowing it to finally pass on to its next plane of existence, and at the same time we're transforming into one being, soon to become the seventh master angel."

Startled by knowing that soon we'll become one being, Amber and I are very worried that we'll lose our own individuality. "Seth, what will happen to us? Are we going to remember anything of our human selves? Will I remember you?" Amber is very worried. "I do not know, Amber, but we cannot fight our path. This was meant to happen to us and we must go along with what Gabriel wants," I answer.

Gabriel steps into the center of Stonehenge and begins to absorb the universal energy, just as he did at the great pyramid, getting stronger and more independent with each passing moment.

"Don't be afraid," he says. "Feel what I'm feeling. This is a wonderful experience!"

Gabriel's thoughts come to us as he finishes his meditation.

He wastes no time in teleporting to the ruins of Tulum. "Amber, this is it. This is the last place," I say. I don't hear anything. Amber is gone. She has let go of herself.

I hear Gabriel's thoughts. "Seth, you must let go of everything that you know and trust me as I absorb the energy from this place. I'll travel to all the ancient sites that are holding this magical energy, but I can't go any further as Gabriel. I must allow myself to transform. You know that Amber has let go. She's now exists totally as spiritual energy.

"Seth, remember when you were in the Golden City looking at the six master angels?"

"Yes, and I saw one empty place. Is that the place for the seventh master angel?"

"That's right. And I'm the being that will transform into that angel. But I can't do that unless you let everything go and allow yourself to become one with spiritual light."

I didn't think I was going to lose my individuality by becoming an angel, but I finally understand that individuality is a human trait. As Gabriel transforms into the seventh master angel, he will become one with spiritual light and the comic being, uniting all things together once again.

A soothing felling comes over me as Gabriel begins to absorb the energy of Tulum. I feel like I'm slipping into unconsciousness.

"Seth, let go of everything. Where you're going there's no need for individuality. You'll become connected to the great plane of deity. It's time. You must allow this to happen," Gabriel says. My last bit of consciousness fades as Gabriel's words fill my body with comfort. I know I can finally let go of everything and allow life to take its natural path.

Gabriel is now in a full, altered state of consciousness, deep in meditation, as he absorbs the universal energy from Tulum.

He slowly transforms, connecting with the cosmic being. A brilliant light begins to flow through him like water flowing down a gentle stream. Wings of light form at his back.

"Gabriel, let go. It's your turn to let go," a voice appears out of nowhere.

Gabriel opens his eyes for the last time as his individual self, and knows that the wise words come from his new self - the seventh master angel.

As he also slips into unconsciousness, surrendering his individuality, Jacob is born and the universal cycle continues.

Date ________________________________

Title ________________________________

Feeling ________________________________

Date ______________________________

Title ______________________________

Feeling ______________________________

Date ________________________________

Title ________________________________

Feeling ________________________________

Date ______________________________

Title ______________________________

Feeling ______________________________

Date ____________________________

Title ____________________________

Feeling ____________________________

Date ______________________________

Title ______________________________

Feeling ______________________________

Date ______________________________

Title ______________________________

Feeling ______________________________

Date ______________________________

Title ______________________________

Feeling ______________________________

Date ________________________________
Title ________________________________
Feeling ________________________________

Date ____

Title ____

Feeling ____

Date ______________________________
Title ______________________________
Feeling ______________________________

Date ______________________________

Title ______________________________

Feeling ______________________________

Date ________________________________

Title ________________________________

Feeling ________________________________

Date ______________________________

Title ______________________________

Feeling ______________________________

Date ______________________________

Title ______________________________

Feeling ______________________________

Date ______________________________

Title ______________________________

Feeling ______________________________

Date ______________________________

Title ______________________________

Feeling ______________________________

Date ______________________________

Title ______________________________

Feeling ______________________________

Date ______________________________

Title ______________________________

Feeling ______________________________

Date ______________________________

Title ______________________________

Feeling ______________________________

Date ______________________________

Title ______________________________

Feeling ______________________________

Date ______________________________

Title ______________________________

Feeling ______________________________

Date ______________________________

Title ______________________________

Feeling ______________________________

Date ______________________________

Title ______________________________

Feeling ______________________________

Date ______________________________

Title ______________________________

Feeling ______________________________

Date ______________________________

Title ______________________________

Feeling ______________________________

Date ______________________________

Title ______________________________

Feeling ______________________________

Date ______________________________

Title ______________________________

Feeling ______________________________

Date ______________________________

Title ______________________________

Feeling ______________________________

Date ______________________________

Title ______________________________

Feeling ______________________________

Date ______________________________

Title ______________________________

Feeling ______________________________

Date ______________________________

Title ______________________________

Feeling ______________________________

Printed in the United States
by Baker & Taylor Publisher Services